North American
Canoe Country

esler-Lampert *Minnesota Heritage* Book Series

This series is published with the generous assistance of he John K. and Elsie Lampert Fesler Fund and David R. and Elizabeth P. Fesler. Its mission is to republish significant out-of-print books that contribute to our understanding and appreciation of Minnesota and the Upper Midwest.

Portage into the Past: By Canoe along the Minnesota-Ontario Boundary Waters by J. Arnold Bolz

The Gift of the Deer by Helen Hoover

The Long-Shadowed Forest by Helen Hoover

A Place in the Woods by Helen Hoover

The Years of the Forest by Helen Hoover

Canoe Country and Snowshoe Country by Florence Page Jaques

North Star Country by Meridel Le Sueur

Lake Superior by Grace Lee Nute

Listening Point by Sigurd F. Olson

The Lonely Land by Sigurd F. Olson

Of Time and Place by Sigurd F. Olson

Open Horizons by Sigurd F. Olson

Reflections from the North Country by Sigurd F. Olson

Runes of the North by Sigurd F. Olson

The Singing Wilderness by Sigurd F. Olson

North American Canoe Country: The Classic Guide to Canoe Technique by Calvin Rutstrum

Voyageur Country: The Story of Minnesota's National Park by Robert Treuer

CALVIN RUTSTRUM

North American Canoe Country

The Classic Guide to Canoe Technique

ILLUSTRATED BY LES KOUBA

University of Minnesota Press
MINNEAPOLIS

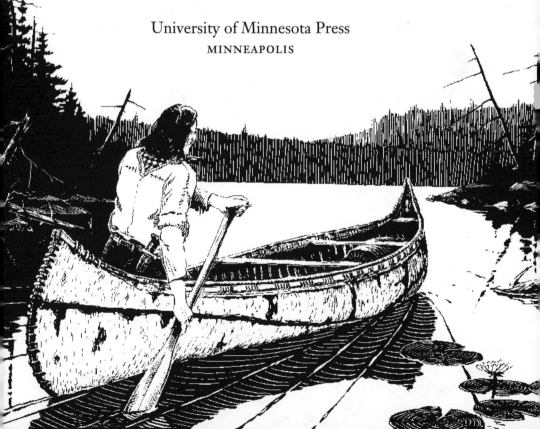

Originally published in hardcover by The Macmillan Company, 1964.
Republished by arrangement with Scribner, an imprint of
Simon & Schuster Inc.

First University of Minnesota Press edition, 2000

Published by the University of Minnesota Press
111 Third Avenue South, Suite 290
Minneapolis, MN 55401-2520
http://www.upress.umn.edu

A Cataloging-in-Publication record for this book is available
from the Library of Congress.

ISBN 0-8166-3660-5

Printed in the United States of America on acid-free paper

The University of Minnesota is an equal-opportunity
educator and employer.

11 10 09 08 07 06 05 04 03 02 01 00   10 9 8 7 6 5 4 3 2 1

TO FLORENCE, MY BETTER HALF,
WHO AS TEMPERING INFLUENCE AND AMANUENSIS
IS GENERALLY WELL ORIENTED,
BUT WHO IS ALWAYS 180 DEGREES OFF COURSE
IN THE WILDERNESS.

CONTENTS

1 ENDLESS WATERS

EXPLORERS, newly arrived on the coast of North America, exclaimed in their first reports to Europe: "We can travel at will in the interior with the craft of the savage."

Ironically, after crossing oceans, white men had no satisfactory means of navigation through the complex water routes of the continent. It was when they met with the primitive people that they learned of a highly mobile form of transportation—the birchbark canoe, ingeniously adapted to land-broken stretches of lakes and rivers. If

1

we contemplate standing on the shores of North America, which had known only primitive man, we realize the magnitude of the undertaking the early explorers faced, and what a welcome expedience the birchbark canoe afforded them.

A single glance at a relief map of the continent reveals a vast and complex network of waterways that almost defies imagination in its uniqueness of pattern. (In one comparatively small area of western Alberta, for example, rivers flow to three oceans—the Pacific, the Atlantic, and the Arctic.) Perhaps the most arresting feature is the narrowness of watersheds, which allowed water systems to be linked in wilderness areas by portage trails and the "craft of the savage."

"The Committee's Punch Bowl," a tiny lake at the summit of the Athabasca Pass, is a classic example of narrow watersheds. From this geographical pinpoint of water, two rivers flow into separate oceans. The Whirlpool River leaves the "Bowl" and flows into the Athabasca River, and eventually into the Mackenzie River to enter the Arctic Ocean. The Wood River leaves the "Bowl" and flows into the Columbia River to enter the Pacific Ocean. This little lake was named by the famous George Simpson, Governor of the Hudson's Bay Company, to honor the Company's committee.

A significant factor in the early development of the area was the unusually narrow watershed between the Hudson and St. Lawrence rivers. This watershed formed a veritable gateway by canoe from the East to the adventure-ridden North, and to the rapidly developing lands to the south.

A bird's-eye view of the continent's waterways shows

"The Committee's Punch Bowl"

that the interior of the continent east of the Rocky Mountains is drained by five main systems: the Mississippi River Valley and its tributaries, the Great Lakes through the St. Lawrence River, the rivers flowing into Hudson Bay, the waters drained by the Mackenzie River, and the Yukon basin. Other watersheds, such as the Colorado, Rio Grande, and Columbia, significant but smaller in scope, drain more local areas.

The water systems in general, their narrow watersheds and contiguous canoe routes, were thus extremely valuable in early exploration and development, providing important trade and social communication between large areas that would otherwise be isolated. These convenient land-and-water arrangements are most fortuitous for the present-day canoe voyager, as they lend insight into the great pattern of canoe travel available to primitive man, and offer clues regarding his ethnic distribution.

Watersheds possess their own special charm. We may suppose that orderliness of natural drainage is purely a physical, gravitational matter, that water must simply run downhill—and so it does. But one cannot help but ponder the complexity of natural drainage, especially after traveling for weeks across Canada's rockbound lakes, around their myriad islands, points, bays, and rivers. How the waters from this complex pattern of lakes, tenuous and lake-expansive rivers could possibly reach the sea, almost defies belief.

If we are not made conscious of the movement of water as we travel by canoe over large and small lakes, we become acutely aware of it when a waterway drops at one end, or even in some unexpected bay, into a roaring cauldron, only to level off again into another lake; or, frequently, assumes the course of a well-channeled river for many miles. The river may wander with the placidness of a lazy stream, spread aimlessly through wild rice beds, and then as unpredictably merge again to charge with thunderous fury over a half dozen or more waterfalls and rapids.

And to confound the mind further, in Canada's Manitoba wilderness there is the Echimamish River, whose name in Cree means "The river that flows both ways."

Or, still another of Nature's baffling complements—Reversible Falls flows in one direction when the tide comes in, and reverses itself when the tide goes out.

Charge with Thunderous Fury Over . . . Waterfalls and Rapids

Examining these strange, natural wonders of North American canoe country, one suddenly becomes aware that he has been saying "up North," when he should have said "*down* North," to describe the flow of rivers heading for the Arctic, or many of those which flow into Hudson Bay.

If the plight of the first voyagers seems awesome just to imagine, we truly begin to comprehend their great adventure when we journey into wilderness lakes that require days on end to cross with canoe and paddle.

We have all learned about the large bodies of water accessible by train or automobile. But strange to most of us are such wilderness lakes in Canada as Dubawnt, Baker, Contwoyto, Clinton-Colden, Wollaston, Reindeer, Ferguson, Michikamau, Nueltin—lakes scarcely touched by white men; water areas whose far shores are mysterious and remote; waters capable of heaving like the sea.

As mystifying and adventure-inspiring as these lakes are the wilderness rivers of Canada and Alaska, whose names have fallen upon few ears: Hay, Severn, Attawapiskat, Moose, Peel, North and South Nahanni, Thelon, Back, Kaniapiskau, Hamilton, Sachigo, Thlewiaza, Yukon, Tanana, Kuskokwim, and numerous others, running through vast forest, tundra, and mountain terrain; rivers brawling with cascades and falls, captivating in their length, overwhelming in their size and flow.

The more settled rivers of the Eastern United States— the Mississippi River system, including the Missouri; the slow-moving waters of the Everglades of the South; the extremely high and low water levels of the Rio Grande; the clear waters of the Columbia; or even the mighty torrents of the Colorado—all in their own way hold out a lifetime of opportunities for canoe travel and study.

Anyone bent on resolving some of the perplexities of Nature can achieve much on a canoe trip, even on a tiny stream that meanders through farming countryside. Whenever I cross a stream deep enough for a canoe, I am tempted to follow its slow, leisurely course. The charm of these local canoe jaunts, the wildlife they reveal, the patterns of Nature they unfold to the curious mind, make even this specialized kind of canoeing fascinating. And such streams are numerous on the North American continent, forming the network for most drainage. In farming areas they often run through woodlots and pastureland, harboring a variety of vegetation, bird, and other animal life. In semisettled regions these streams lead unexpectedly into interesting areas of forest, lake, and marshland. In the remote wilderness, they are among the least explored regions of the world, and contain some of the greatest undiscovered natural phenomena.

The canoe country of North America includes a great deal more than remote wilderness areas. For, in addition to being enjoyable, canoe travel can often have a constructive and scholarly purpose. A lifetime of research can be devoted to one river alone, such as the Susquehanna, Potomac, Hudson, St. Croix, Rio Grande, or a hundred other rivers in the more settled regions, without exhausting their historic, scientific, and recreational advantages.

Too often, these rivers are given consideration only by local people. But the National Audubon Society, the National Geographic Society, and other natural history organizations, along with enterprising individuals and groups, are increasing the importance of these areas for both general and specialized study.

"Float trips," down the Mississippi, the Missouri, and

A Huckleberry Finn Contrivance for Float Trips

tributary rivers, have become popular. Generally, the trips are made with shallow-draft boats, but two canoes with a platform of boards laid across them, a tent pitched on the platform—a sort of Huckleberry Finn contrivance—is a method appearing more and more frequently along United States and Canadian rivers. It has come into particular favor with the Indians and white settlers along the Mackenzie and tributary rivers, which have the kind of flow appropriate to the dual canoe arrangement.

The Great Lakes, despite their immense and perilous water areas, have become increasingly attractive as canoe water. And while the ever-present hazards of big seas should never be underestimated, they may be minimized by the experienced canoe traveler who knows the special risks. Generally, the greatest hazard is to be caught in a running sea behind long stretches of bold cliff, where escape to shore is not always possible.

We may be sure that the early canoe explorers from the Saguenay to the Rocky Mountains were not deterred by the imposing vastness of the Great Lakes. Duluth (Du Lhut), La Vérendrye, and a host of other intrepid and distinguished explorers, along with members of the fur trade, plied their paddles in the heavy-running seas of Lake Superior and other big lakes, such as Great Bear, Athabasca, and Slave far to the north.

Some years ago I covered more than a hundred miles of Lake Superior's north shore alone in a canoe, from about the Pigeon River to the Slate Islands, in an effort, if possible, to capture something of what the early explorers experienced as they threaded their way through the alluring wilderness archipelago of Canada's Lake Superior north shore waters. The magnificent wilderness, I found, is still there, left almost inviolate, with a good population of wildlife remaining—even a small band of caribou on the Slate Islands.

As we consider canoe travel in the United States, two main regions are most often suggested: Maine and Minnesota. With similar rivers and connecting lakes, coniferous forests, and comparable seasons, Maine and Minnesota are much alike. Many other regions in the United States have significant and excellent canoe routes, but are more populated or more limited in scope.

In Minnesota lies the Superior National Forest, joining Canada's Quetico Provincial Park. Here are the canoe waters which have been caught in a legal squeeze by an oppressive force, whose exploits have sought to commercialize the area with roads, jukeboxes, and general ravage

Caribou on Some of the Islands

of fish and wildlife, but fortunately have failed. The fight against these destructive forces began in President Teddy Roosevelt's time, when this area was set aside as a wilderness domain.

The latest phase of a broad, successful program to save the region, following the restriction against roads, has been the banning of the airplane. Constant vigilance must be maintained, and presidential proclamation followed by legislative act, if the Superior National Forest is to remain a wilderness canoe water area for future generations.

What constructive program the state of Maine will manage to continue in the years ahead for the preservation of its canoe country, time and the foresight of her own people will determine.

Both Maine and Minnesota have areas of rockbound lakes and rivers, by nature unsuitable for agriculture, but nevertheless enriched with heavy forests of spruce, balsam, pine, birch, and poplar. So numerous are the lakes and connecting rivers that canoe routes may be selected in almost any direction.

The Superior National Forest is a part of the two million square miles of Pre-Cambrian or Laurentian Shield— a horseshoe-shaped region of ancient rock, encircling Hudson Bay, and comprising more than half of Canada.

The two million square miles of the Shield, which, like the Superior National Forest, are unsuitable for agriculture, promise to remain a permanent wilderness. The Shield's forests and minerals are objects of exploitation, but a day will come when the deposits are exhausted. Already the forests are being regulated by a system of controlled cutting and planting to make them perpetual. Fringes of the forest have been found to supply ample pulpwood needs, so that remote areas no longer need be invaded. Fur farms and synthetically manufactured fur are cutting back on trapping. The number of fur-bearing animals is thus steadily increasing along canoe routes. Waterfalls in the remote wilderness areas have now a good chance of remaining inviolate, since electric power has become more economical when generated by atomic fuel at the site where it is consumed.

Canada and Alaska thus hold great permanent promise for the lusty individual who aspires to travel by canoe through a deep wilderness. It is in the Pre-Cambrian or Laurentian Shield and much of Alaska that the nature of the terrain will probably permit endurance of the greatest wilderness adventures and opportunities for wildlife observation.

We need only take a look at a map of Canada, one of the large land masses in the world, to appreciate the magnitude of the promise it holds for the canoe voyager.

Moving inland from the Atlantic Coast, the watershed spills the Eastmain, Rupert, Broadback, Missisicabi, Fort George, Nottaway, Big and Little Whale rivers, and a host of others, into Hudson Bay. These rivers, also on the Pre-Cambrian Shield, flow in their almost changeless beds of solid rock, responding to every caprice of the rocky terrain to form a magnificent succession of rapids and falls. At other intervals they calmly and leisurely wind as long stretches of well-behaved rivers, expanding into lake or widening marsh. These variations continue through a virtually untouched wilderness, until the rivers reach the semisalt waters of Hudson Bay.

To the south and west of Hudson Bay—surrounded by the Bay on the one side and the Pre-Cambrian Shield on the other—is the Hudson Bay lowland, a strip of clay that changes the whole nature of the rivers here.

The sources of the lowland rivers to a large extent lie in the Pre-Cambrian Shield, and there offer the canoe voyager magnificent coniferous forests, rockbound shores, intermittent lakes, and generally rugged terrain. But about halfway or less down these rivers, the route enters the utter flatness of the clay belt from Churchill—with its permafrost, sparse forest growth—on the north, to the Harricanaw River in the dense spruce forests on the south.

The entire northeastern portion of Canada, extending from a southwest boundary, roughly on a line from Churchill on Hudson Bay to northern Alaska, comprises the treeless, permafrost Arctic tundra, and includes the large group of islands reaching almost to the North Pole.

Through this tundra region of the mainland flow the famous Coppermine, Back, Colville, and Arctic Red rivers of exploration history, emptying into their respective bays of the Arctic Ocean. The tundra has attracted canoe expeditions for study of the Eskimo; of the nesting grounds of migratory birds; and for observation of the annual migration of the caribou herd.

Like other regions of Canada, the tundra lures the prospector, the explorer, and the general adventurer; and it rarely fails to capture the romantic spirit, despite its falsely reputed austerity. Like the Southwest desert areas, it is a living and challenging natural wonder: but unlike the dry-tropical and Lower Sonoran life zones of the Southwest desert, the tundra—in spite of its low, flat nature—compares in growth with the arctic-alpine life zones above the tree line of mountains farther south.

The western part of the Northwest Territories contains the famous Mackenzie River, the longest river in Canada, lying well outside the tundra. It begins at Great Slave Lake, and drains a number of historically exciting rivers from the south—the Athabasca, Peace, Hay, Liard, and others, all superb canoe routes.

To the west of the Mackenzie lies the Pacific coastal area, a 400-mile-wide mountainous strip, whose rugged rivers offer perhaps a greater challenge for the canoe voyager than any other part of the continent. Here, the most ambitious can find their skill and endurance put to severe tests in mountain rivers.

In this region of the Yukon Territory and western part of the District of Mackenzie, we swing off to the west and bridge another famous watershed, leaving the rivers which have taken us through the vast Mackenzie River basin from the south. Now, over small water and rather difficult portage trails, we pick up the streams that lead into the traditionally famous Yukon River, through the broad reaches of Alaska to Norton Sound in the Bering Sea—where water again meets water, endlessly.

2 THE CANOE—WHAT IS IT?

IT IS technically difficult to define "canoe." Dictionaries define it as "a long, narrow boat pointed at both ends, and propelled by paddles." But a definition so broad could include kayaks, dugouts, and a variety of boats combining similar features. We think of a canoe as a craft that must be not only "long, narrow, and pointed at both ends," but also light enough to be carried over portages on the shoulders of one man (or several men, depending on the size of the canoe), and also be capable of carrying men and their equipment effectively over a variety of inland waters. For safe travel in rough water the craft should have a load capacity of approximately twelve times its own weight, allowing at least six inches of freeboard. (Freeboard is the distance from the water to the gunwale.)

A careful study of the best canoe design shows that a craft that is light enough to be carried over portage trails and most efficient in rough water must not be encumbered with extraneous parts or needless weight in the design of the hull. Thus, it seems strange that most canoes—including the Indian's bark canoe—while they give fairly satisfactory service, do not follow the best basic principle of design. This is not a capricious choice, but a scientific matter of providing, through design and practical weight, the greatest safety against heavy-running seas and rough rapids. The drawing below demonstrates this principle.

In defining the basic canoe concept, I prefer to omit the kayak from the canoe category, because the kayak is a craft distinct from the canoe, and has its own set of principles. It is commendable for its particular purpose, but is designed primarily for sea hunting, not for long-distance travel with heavy, bulky loads over water and portage trails. Although the kayak is sometimes used inland, a totally different craft, the umiak, was adapted by the arctic Eskimo for extensive travel with heavy loads. The umiak is a raw-skin-covered boat, 20 to 30 feet long and 6 to 8 feet wide. It is used on the tundra rivers, but its chief function is transporting families along the arctic coastal regions.

Commercial adaptations of the Eskimo kayak, made of wood and metal, with a plastic covering, have come onto the market. They are much heavier than the Eskimo's, and are usually made in takedown form, so that they can be carried in the trunk of a car. Where a wilderness journey requires travel by pack horse to a watercourse, this unit may be used in place of the canoe. It does well in rapids

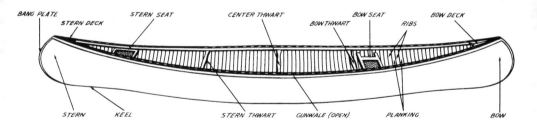

Canoe Nomenclature

Eskimo Kayak

because it is decked over like the original Eskimo kayak, and some unusual feats have been performed with it in the rapids of the Colorado River and other tumultuous waters. However, the same decked-over principle can be applied to the canoe by providing a snap cover with openings for the paddlers, as in the kayak. The serious shortcomings of the commercial kayak are the lack of storage space for equipment and provisions and the craft's increased weight.

The "dugout," of course, is significant and worthy of mention. Regarded as a canoe in early wilderness travel, it was soon eliminated from the common category of canoes because of its heavy weight. Made in a single piece from a large log, the tree for the dugout log was felled and hollowed out by controlled burning. The fire was extinguished periodically, and the resulting burned charcoal layer hacked and scraped away with stone, ivory, or bone tools. Later dugouts were created with steel tools, the felling done with axes and saws, the hollowing-out work performed with a lip-faced adze, ax, wedge, gouge, or specially improvised handmade tools.

Where preserved dugouts are on exhibit, it is sometimes suggested that an enormous log, equivalent in diameter to the width of the dugout, was used in its construction. This is incorrect. The surprising beam width in these dugouts was achieved by using the smallest working opening through which the hollowing-out process could be accomplished in order to retain the greatest possible wall area of the log for later expansion. This expansion was accomplished by filling the hollowed-out log with water heated by immersing hot stones; the walls were then sprung out to the desired beam width and secured in this position by thwart braces. The expansive pressure of the water was generally sufficient after prolonged soaking to force the walls into the desired position. If not, boulders were added to increase the pressure, helped also by manual prying.

Perhaps the strangest aspect of the construction was the boring of numerous holes in the unfinished hull in order to gauge its thickness. When the craft was finished, these holes were closed with plugs of wood.

The beautifully decorated Kwakiutl canoes of the Canadian West Coast Indians were undoubtedly in art and craftsmanship the finest specimens of the dugout ever created. (See illustration.)

Watercraft made with light frames of wood, covered with parchment (untanned animal skins) have appeared in various parts of the world in a variety of forms. The Eskimo's kayak is perhaps one of the best. The Cree's parchment craft, called an upinoose, was an open-top, canoelike vessel, having features of both canoe and boat.

The most radical deviation from the basic canoe design is the Kootenay canoe. Its distribution is limited largely to the Kootenay region of British Columbia and the adjoining area in the United States. The shell is made of western white pine bark, a bark more adaptable to the making of this craft than the coarser bark of the eastern white pine. A few are made of birch bark.

The unusual aspect of the design is that the bow and the stern are formed into cones. (See illustration.) The first impression one gets is that a long, keel-like section hangs heavily below the water surface. But the background drawing shows that the points of the keel at the bow and stern curve up, very slightly above the water. The keel is not built on what appears to be a straight line, but is quite similar to the keel curve of the common canoe.

The Dugout

FINAL WIDTH OF CANOE AFTER THWARTS FORCE SIDES OUTWARD

DIAM. OF TREE

The Kwakiutl Dugout

If we study the dotted lines shown in the illustration to compare the general lines of the Kootenay canoe with the average Guide's model canoe, we see that a great deal of seemingly unnecessary material has in theory been removed from the bow and stern in the Kootenay to reduce the weight, while still retaining a high load capacity. Actually, the portions in the illustration theoretically removed from the Guide's model are not entirely extraneous, and therefore the Kootenay design has not quite reached the highest possible efficiency in load capacity for canoe

The Kootenay Canoe

weight. Nevertheless, it is a unique design, noteworthy for its unusual lightness relative to weight-carrying capacity, though lacking somewhat in bulk capacity.

The Kootenay canoe does have proved safety advantages in running rapids and heavy seas. The closed, cone-shaped bow and stern, alternately dipping under water and coming out in the rise and fall of heavy waves and rapids, create the buoyancy which produces its traditionally safe freeboard. Thus, in principle, the Kootenay has some of the safety advantages of the kayak. The upper parts of the conelike bow and stern are wedge-edged so the bow and stern can, by literally parting the water, emerge readily from their submerged plunges without much resistance.

Most models of the Kootenay canoe, which I used for experiment, disclosed its strong points. One difficulty I did find in the design is that the paddlers must sit rather far from the bow or the stern, and this more central paddling position reduces maneuverability. I believe that commercial canoe manufacturers could adopt the Kootenay design as a valuable lightweight canoe model, by moving the paddler positions closer to the bow and the stern and reinforcing the apex of the conical bow and stern, especially the more vulnerable bow. The Kootenay design has great commercial possibilities, because it is very seaworthy. The unusual shape naturally requires a visual adjustment for those who are accustomed to the conventional canoe model.

The craft that was traditionally destined to become the symbol of exploration, the one best adapted to the white man's exploration of the wilderness of North America, was what the Cree called a "wuskwiecheman"; the French, "betulinus linter"; the English, "birchbark canoe."

The largest of the birchbarks was a craft of no small proportions compared with our modern recreational canoe. Thirty-six feet long, 5 feet wide at the beam, and 2 feet or more in depth, it became known to the French *voyageur* as the *Maître* (master); to the English as the Montreal.

It seems incredible to us in our industrial age that a craft made of such seemingly fragile materials as birch bark and cedar, bound together with spruce or tamarack roots (watap), the seams filled with a heated mixture of resin, charcoal, and fat, could possibly be strong enough to carry the huge loads of freight and men that plied the watercourses between Montreal and the inland fur center of

The Montreal Canoe

Grand Portage—a rugged round trip made in the open water in a single season.

The strength of the birchbark craft lay, of course, in its high resiliency. With the natural repair materials of birch bark, resins, and fat at hand on nearly every forest shore, maintenance of these canoes was rather simple and routine. (The resin or pitch compound used on the birchbark seams was made by heating a mixture of six part of resins from cone-bearing trees, one part of animal fat, and pulverized charcoal. The fat gave the resin plasticity; the charcoal, body.)

For the inland waterways above Lake Superior, a canoe with considerably less capacity than the Montreal was used—the North. The next size smaller than the North was called the bastard, because it was not up to the standard of the North and was bigger than the smallest of the birchbarks, the so-called *Indian*. The *Indian* was the canoe of the solitary Indian trapper, who sought his pelts and game over the devious, secluded routes of streams and inland waterways.

From these four basic models come the commercial canoes of our time: wood, wood-and-canvas, aluminum, magnesium, plastic-impregnated wood, and canoes made with Fiberglas mats bonded with plastic.

The Canoe Principles

An examination of the technical aspects of the canoe principle shows that, as I have suggested, most canoes, including the birchbarks and the commercial canoes, have not been designed in the most practical and efficient way.

This basic principle is that to reach its greatest carrying capacity over rough water with the least weight on the portages, a canoe should be designed to have the best possible freeboard areas when the bow and stern are plunging through heavy seas or the white water of rapids —not, certainly, a freeboard area suited only to calm seas or smooth streams.

The chief difficulty in achieving this ideal design is in determining the proper curve of gunwale and the best width for buoyancy of bow and stern. In the illustration of the Montreal birchbark canoe, you can see that the gunwale runs parallel to a dead waterline. The dangerous canoe routes through the Great Lakes became even more hazardous with these canoes because the flat gunwales lacked sufficient freeboard in the proper areas—somewhat back from the bow and forward of the stern—*specifically those freeboard areas that plunge deepest as the canoe pitches through heavy seas.* (See illustrative sketch showing shape of gunwales as they apply to proper and improper distribution of freeboard areas.)

As a canoe pitches through rough water, with its bow and stern mounting and plunging, the fulcrum or pivot is at the widest part, the beam or center, sometimes called the "waist." It will be clear, on studying the illustration of the canoe running a heavy sea, that as the bow and the stern alternately plunge to their lowest depths, water will spill into an improperly constructed canoe a short distance back from the bow, and just forward of the stern, not, as generally presumed, over the bow or stern, nor at the center of the canoe. Thus, we can determine that a canoe loaded to full capacity and riding the heaviest sea possible must have a maximum submersion freeboard waterline as it plunges, which is still safely above the water when the bow and the stern dip to their deepest submersion points.

Any construction that extends freeboard areas far above any possible submersion point such as sharply upturned bows and sterns is extraneous, and a lack of freeboard area where it is needed is obviously bad canoe design. Extraneous parts and freeboard areas, created through poor design, only add excess weight on the portages.

The traditional and symbolically decorated upsweeps of the bow and stern of the Montreal birchbark canoes lent charm but not added buoyancy on heavy seas. They did, however, have one valuable function on land. As the canoe lay in camp, bottom up, it was poised with a three-point suspension—the upsweeps of the bow, stern, and one gunwale—so as to give access to the underside of the canoe for shelter—usually the only ready roof over the *voyageurs'* heads.

Gunwales varied somewhat on the Montreal and the North canoes over the years, but they remained rather flat throughout the period of the fur trade, never fully reaching the best design for highest efficiency as we have learned to recognize it today through advanced marine engineering and modern practical application.

Diagram Showing Proper and Improper Gunwale

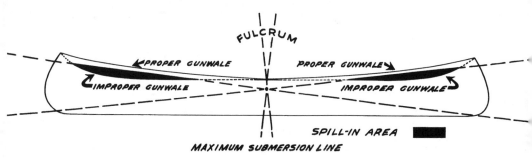

Running a Heavy Sea—Showing Freeboard Area

When commercial canoes of wood, wood and canvas, metal, and plastic began reaching the market, pattern of gunwales, curvature of bilges, fullness and taper of bow and stern, and design in general began to improve. But comparatively few of these commercial canoes have reached design and technically balanced proportions that would give the highest efficiency in heavy seas and allow minimum weight for portaging. Flat gunwales, sharply turned-up ends, narrow bow and stern, and badly shaped bilges have continued to dominate most canoe design, producing vessels best suited to city park lakes. The sharp upsweeps of bow and stern deceptively charm the inexperienced eye.

Canoes, which come closest to providing the ideal ratio of load-carrying capacity in rough water in relation to minimum portage weight, have been called, by manufacturers of wood, wood-and-canvas, and metal canoes, the Guide's model and Prospector. These two types, somewhat alike in general principle and design, are best suited to major wilderness canoe travel. They are easily identified by the low, gradually rising bow and stern with a rather low, flat deck. The gunwale lines, when they make a canoe most efficient for rough water, describe, roughly, a shallow segment approximately 30 degrees of a great circle.

Bows and sterns have long been subject to erroneous construction, some too narrow, others too full. The designers of the narrow bows and sterns have mistakenly believed that if these sections were narrow, they would "cut the water." The narrow bow and stern only reduce buoyancy at these points, causing the entire canoe to ride deeper in the water—therefore, more sluggishly. Also, the lack of buoyancy in the bow and stern allows them to plunge dangerously deep in a heavy sea. On the other hand, bows and sterns that are too full result in canoes that do not respond properly to the pitch of rough water, and are sluggish to maneuver. The width of bow and stern which gives the best relative buoyancy is that which will allow a loaded

The Montreal Canoe—Usually the Only Ready Roof over the Voyageurs' Heads

canoe to have a *freeboard waterline nearly parallel to the gunwale when the bow or the stern have plunged to their respective lowest points in rough water.* This principle is illustrated in the diagram and in the artist's sketch of a canoe riding a heavy sea.

Fiberglas-plastic canoes are produced by a number of firms. Properly designed Guide's and Prospector models in this material may reach the market soon. In the past, Fiberglas-plastic material proved too heavy for canoes of wilderness cruising capacity, but new models with less plastic and more efficient Fiberglas construction—resulting in lighter crafts—are being developed.

To date, the lightest canoes for their size are made of

aluminum. These canoes are furnished in standard and lightweight models. Styrofoam safety compartments or air chambers are created at both ends under the decks for buoyancy in the event of an upset. The original aluminum canoe models of too light weight did not stand up well. Seats tended to draw in the gunwales and break them down. But this has now been corrected by adding material support to the weak areas. Competition in aluminum canoes is growing, and the buyer should explore the general market for the canoe of his choice, carefully examining comparative structural principles. Not all aluminum canoes made by one manufacturer are designed efficiently. Some are still modeled after the extreme upturn of bow and stern on canoes used in city parks. Therefore, careful distinction for wilderness travel should be made in choosing the Prospector or the Guide's model described, in the aluminum, wood, wood-and-canvas, and Fiberglas-plastic canoes.

The 18-foot-length, lightweight aluminum canoe is practical for general wilderness travel if the rapids to be run are not unusually rough or the lake too large. The 13- and 15-foot aluminum canoes are so short in relation to their beam that they are too easily thrown off keel, and have a poor pitch in rough water. When carrying normal loads, they paddle sluggishly. Many people believe that the shorter canoes save much labor on the portages, but the difference in weight between them and the 18-foot, lightweight aluminum canoe is negligible considering the low submersion level and the paddling drag of the shorter canoes. With modern lightness of canoes, it is better to select one with a capacity somewhat greater than is actually needed. Larger canoes ride higher and move faster with the same paddling energy. In heavy waves and rapids, the larger canoes, of course, have a distinct safety advantage.

An excellent example of how buoyancy varies in relation to weight and carrying capacity is shown in the following figures of one manufacturer's 15-foot and 18-foot canoes in the lightweight models: Weight of 15-foot canoe, 55 pounds; carrying capacity, 905 pounds. Weight of 18-foot canoe, 67 pounds; carrying capacity, 1,158 pounds. Thus, increasing the weight of the canoe itself by 12 pounds increases the carrying capacity by 253 pounds. In short, the 18-foot canoe has been raised well out of the water, giving approximately eleven pounds of increased carrying capacity for every pound that was added to the weight of the canoe. This obviously means greater buoyancy. The 18-foot canoe is going to ride much higher and, therefore, with a great deal less resistance to the water than the 13-, 15- and 17-foot canoes when the equipment and provision load is the same and even to a certain degree heavier.

The all-wood cedar canoes, more prominently used in the early part of the century, are delightful. I have warm feelings also for the wood-and-canvas models. If an aluminum violin gave you the same mellow tone as a Stradivarius, you would undoubtedly still object to an aluminum violin and take the wooden Stradivarius. While I use aluminum canoes too, the sentiment I have for the wood and wood-and-canvas canoes lingers. Furthermore, the aluminum canoe is a noisy craft for observing and photographing wildlife.

On the other hand, in canoes of a given size, the wood-and-canvas canoes, even when new and dry, are much heavier than the aluminum. And when the wood-and-canvas canoes have been on the wilderness trail in several rains, they weigh even more. Nevertheless, I hope they will long endure.

Although some aluminum canoes are treated and painted for decoration or to reduce glare, they actually require no refinishing or service beyond accident repairs, and no storage protection from the weather. They can be repaired on the trail with a gum patch, and welded later. Aluminum canoes should not be used in salt water unless primed and painted inside and out. Salt-water oxidation destroys aluminum.

The Square Stern Canoe

> And it floated on the river
> Like a yellow leaf in Autumn,
> Like a yellow water-lily.
>
> —LONGFELLOW

Yes—but where do you put the outboard motor?

Late in the era of canoe development came the canoe with a square stern to accommodate the outboard motor. Traditionalists have suggested that the square stern canoe is neither a canoe nor a boat, deserving the name "bastard" like the early birchbark canoe, previously mentioned.

But like it or not, it has established its uses. Heavy freighting canoes are made both with square sterns and pointed ends, but the square sterns predominate. The large wood-and-canvas freighting canoes are 22 feet long, and have a capacity of 5,000 pounds. The largest aluminum freighting canoe is made in 19-foot length for square stern, capacity 1,550 pounds; and 20-foot length with pointed ends, capacity 1,600 pounds. Canoes as short as 17 feet are now available with square sterns.

The first consideration in the selection of a square stern canoe is to make sure that the flat face of the transom does not continue below the waterline. Some aluminum canoes have this serious defect, and the manufacturers should lose no time in correcting it. The flat area of the transom below the water creates a drag, kicks up a swirl, and back-whips water into the canoe with motor speed. When paddling the canoe, the flat area below the water creates a noisy suction churn, thus making the canoe entirely unfit for the quiet travel essential in wildlife photography, hunting, and observing wildlife. The silent underwater stroke has no value when using a below-waterline transom canoe. (See illustration of Improper Square Stern—Proper Square Stern.)

Paddling or freighting canoes, pointed at both ends, designed only for paddling, can be provided with brackets to accommodate outboard motors, operated at the rear left. This may seem to be an improvisation of the square stern, but it is in some ways an improvement. Whereas a boat has a wide transom, which allows the operator to sit to one side of the steering arm, the square stern canoe holds the motor awkwardly accessible behind the operator, and even when the steering arm is extended and cocked off to one side, it is not convenient. In the bracket-application motor-support, the operator has a comfortable position, with the steering arm conveniently at his side.

Perhaps the biggest objection to the square-stern motor-application is the terrific impact on the operator's spinal column as he sits at the extreme rear, and the canoe pitches in a heavy sea. It is comparable to the jolt received while sitting on a toboggan over a rough slide, and is even more painful in canoes with badly constructed transoms that extend below the waterline. In rough water, and particularly in rapids, the operation of a motor on the square stern is not only awkward but hazardous because of the operator's risky sitting position in relation to motor control. Under such conditions, square stern canoe operators will find it more convenient to fix the motor in a forward position with a wrench, by tightening the steering bearing clamp, and then do the steering with a canoe paddle used as a rudder.

A frequent objection to a side bracket is that the canoe is not properly balanced with the offset of the motor. This is easily compensated for in an empty canoe by placing a dead weight as a counterbalance on the wide bottom part of the canoe. In a loaded canoe, of course, the complaint is meaningless because the load can be adjusted to compensate the offset of the relatively light motor. A canoe should

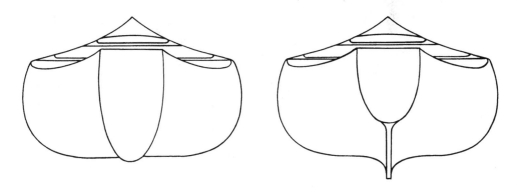

Improper Square Stern (left), **Proper Square Stern** (right)

not have a motor which is too heavy for the size of the canoe. It may be a serious hazard in an upset, and its excessive power can prove dangerous in water with hidden reefs.

In efficiency of operation, the square-stern-mounted motor may seem to be in a position of direct forward drive, while the motor on the side bracket appears to be off center. Any difference in efficiency will be found negligible, since the bracket mount is on the narrow part of the canoe and behind the widest part. This bracket mount is valuable when two motors are needed, as, for example, in a long and precarious run up a mountain river of exceptionally fast water. If one motor should fail, the second assures control of the canoe and a safe landing. Commercial brackets have a taper, allowing the two motors to be mounted in dovetail fashion almost directly across from each other. The bracket for the right side, not being standard, requires reconstruction, which any metalworking shop can do, the needed changes being obvious when the requirements are explained. It is not necessary to synchronize the speed of the two motors. However, if they do run at approximately the same speed, a small added efficiency is achieved.

When traveling with two motors, it is wise to fix one of them in a straightforward position by tightening the steering bearing clamp, and then steer with the other motor. On a 20-foot aluminum Guide's model canoe, I use two 3-horsepower outboard motors. Large freighting canoes in very fast water need larger motors. The dual motor assembly has advantages when the journey is long, and there is a chance that one motor may fail beyond field repair.

3 SELECTING AND PLANNING A CANOE ROUTE

FOR ME, the blank spaces on a map are always the most exciting. Earlier in my canoe travel days, when much of the wilderness had not yet been charted aerially, maps showed rivers well defined in their proper courses for a short distance back from their mouths where they had been explored, then purely conjectural dotted lines were projected into the blank areas of the Unknown. These dotted lines seldom were drawn where they should have been, and in this uncertainty of terrain lay the attraction for the explorer.

Fear of the Unknown is basic in man's nature. Yet the Unknown is also an irresistible lure.

Any amount of labor portaging or tracking a canoe up a succession of rapids seems worthwhile to reveal the mysteries of the "dotted lines." "Why," you ask, "did the party of explorers turn around at this point?" "Was seasonal time a factor?" "Were provisions running low?" "Did misadventure dog their tracks?"

These were the intriguing questions before and upon reaching the "dotted lines." Provision shortage, seasonal difficulties, misadventure—all, I am sure, have added up to halt the voyager. Sometimes exploration ended at a formidable rapid or a canyon with no accessibility to the interior other than long, grueling portages that must literally be cut out with an ax. Perhaps the travelers would have had to track or pole, which would have been foolhardy at threatening times of the year.

Extensive mapping of the wilderness by plane has erased most of the "dotted lines," and placed the rivers on their proper geographical courses. Some of the lure, of course, is gone, but the rivers are still there—much as they always have been. The larger part of the wilderness remains a challenge great enough for the most ambitious canoe voyager.

In the United States, as in Canada, canoe maps are best obtained from government sources, although private map companies in the United States and Canada also can be good sources. Canoe outfitters generally have maps of their own surrounding regions, some on the back of their folders. The United States Army Corps of Engineers has made a lake survey, showing the United States water routes in good detail. These maps are available by writing to the United States Army Lake Survey, Detroit 26, Michigan.

Canadian maps can be obtained from the Department of Lands and Forests, Ottawa, Ontario. The proper procedure is first to write for an index map, which shows each provisional edition map in its respective position, named and numbered. Because this index map covers a large area, you will be able to lay out your entire canoe route on it, and then select the various provisional edition maps required—ordering only those which cover every detailed part of your route. The provisional edition maps are generally made on a scale of 4 miles to the inch; a few, 2 and 8 miles to the inch. They are made from the air by photography and are quite accurate, showing

District boundaries

Pack or portage trails, including winter trails

Survey lines (generally only base and meridian lines)

Rapids and falls with drop in feet

Marsh, bog, and open muskeg

Woods, tundra, and prairie

Buildings, such as cabins (generally fur trading posts and well-established trapping cabins)

Height or elevation of various water levels above the sea, in feet

Declination of the compass in degrees (see chapter on position finding)

Latitude and longitude in degrees and minutes (some only in 15-minute divisions)

Direction of water flow

Individual names of lakes and rivers when they have a name (many are yet unnamed).

While my early travels in unmapped regions were not hit-or-miss ventures, thanks to astronomical instruments and plotted courses, I must admit that life would have been a good deal easier with these maps. Perhaps more romance is to be enjoyed by plotting a course from observations of solar bodies, and coming upon natural surprises.

But even maps, no matter how accurate, do not always provide the easy guide to canoe travel. When you multiply the size of the lakes and rivers on your map to their real size, in a proportion of 1 on paper to 253,440 (1 inch equals 4 miles) on land and water, the route calls for imagination, and in some instances, celestial plotting of position. The resourcefulness of the canoe voyager is called into play too often for the "big adventure" to be written off casually.

Perhaps the most valuable addition to the canoe voyager's material for selecting a route is mimeographed trip sheets, knowledge provided by voyagers who have gone before, and who were thoughtful and generous enough to make accurate records of waterways and portage trails. A great many canoe routes are available in these sheets, which can be obtained from the Canadian Department of Mines and Technical Surveys, Ottawa, Ontario. When we refer to "those who have gone before," we need to take into consideration large numbers of voyagers—government workers, private parties, trappers, traders, et cetera.

Possibly, a far greater library of these mimeographed route records would be available were it not for the esoteric nature of the lone wilderness traveler. He is quite often introverted, an individual who has discovered a route of such magnificence and interest that he guards it with secrecy and, on occasion, deception. He will return to that region only with the hope that he will not meet others.

Whatever we think of these insular-minded people, we should not judge them too harshly. To them the "silent places" are significant only when such places remain inviolate beyond their own solitary travel. Prospectors, too, most often come and go over the deep wilderness routes of the continent, sometimes secretly starting their route in the dead of night, and months later emerging without a word to suggest where they have been.

While these trip sheets are generally good enough to be of service, they are not always infallible. At times, judgment of distance, accuracy of direction, or even exact location has been in error. Not all wilderness travelers have the ability to judge relative water or land areas in their proper proportions or perspective. Islands may easily be taken for points; points for islands; and quite often, islands for straight mainland when they are long and parallel to a shore. A long, narrow strip of water between two islands, or between a long island and the mainland, has on occasion been taken for a river into which a lake flowed. Impressions vary, and the moods of weather, physical well-being, and stress of travel often influence judgment.

Allowances must be made for those who were incapable of identifying what, in all sincerity, they believed to be a visual certainty. Even in the records of prominent early explorers, we see a marked difference in ability to observe accurately. Some voyagers were careful workers and not so easily influenced by the stress of bad weather, heavily running seas, the imminent need for getting into camp, provision shortage, and the many imposing factors faced in wilderness travel. Others were less observant, more acutely affected by the chain of such diverting events.

Use these trip sheets, by all means, but with the reservation of your own judgment. Then, if you do find errors, make sure of your own observations, and correct the errors on the sheets. Those who come after you will benefit, and government records will be improved.

Selecting a canoe route will, of course, be based on such

obvious factors as: time allotted for the trip, the budget, time of year, and physical capabilities of the party members. But I think the most important qualification of the members is their experience as it applies to travel in a particular kind of country and season. Also, there can be a great deal of difference between actual experience and a daredevil attitude of presuming to have it. If hell, as the saying goes, is paved with incompetence and good intentions, then, too, are many lake and river bottoms paved with the equipment of overzealous canoeists, if not also littered with their unfortunate bones.

Common sense will tell us that beginners without guides should not plan trips through water which is too rough for any but veteran canoeists. A good plan at the start is to pick a route that has well-defined portage trails, small lakes, rivers without dangerous rapids, and routes of moderate distance. Such country can be just as much a part of the wilderness as the more adventurous routes. It can offer more leisure for the uninitiated, more chance for reflection upon the merits of the undertaking; but most important, it will add to experience, setting in motion reflexes that will operate more efficiently and bring greater assurance to the next, perhaps major, voyage.

Provisional edition sheets will show the general nature of routes, and the mimeographed records will describe the water and portages sufficiently to lay out almost any kind of a canoe trip.

One geographical phase—water level—cannot be satisfactorily described in maps, and generally is not mentioned in the mimeo sheets. It should be given special consideration. The entire canoe route can change from its normal succession of portages, rapids, and smooth water, either by a season of drought or a season of excessive rain-fall.

A river that was a shallow rapid, described in the mimeo sheet by a canoe party as easy to track with short lines, may, after a season of heavy rainfall, be a roaring cascade that has to be portaged, perhaps over terrain that does not provide a good trail—none having been needed during normal water-level conditions. Sometimes an advantage is gained where unusually high water eliminates the need for a portage, where one is normally indicated. A connecting stream swollen by excessive rainfall may permit paddling the canoe right through. Also, it can be very disappointing to reach a shallow river that was good access water for a canoe in normal or high water, only to find, after a drought, that you have to portage several miles through shallows that are mere meandering trickles, though this is rare. The North does not have the Southwest's recurring arroyos.

It is well to tap every available source for information, both governmental and private. An excellent example of the need for good planning lies in the route from the St. Lawrence River through the Saguenay River to Lake Mistassini and down the Rupert River to Rupert House on James Bay. That part of the route from Lake Mistassini through the upper Rupert River, while having some lake expanses, runs through a difficult series of heavy, thundering rapids and chutes. A lack of knowledge here will send the canoe party over a discouraging course, where the logical route on this trip is a detour through the Marten River, and back into the Rupert River—a distance of about ninety miles, around the rough water.

A further consideration in planning a route is to determine from road and railroad maps of the region whether embarkation points are possible from new road and rail extensions. The Alcan Highway has opened up a great range of canoe routes heretofore inaccessible except by long voyages. New railroad branch lines and often secondary auto roads are being built and extended continually, which may not appear very soon on maps.

Sometimes youth groups or adults with limited experience need to plan a trip which does not take them very far from an auto road or railroad at any point. A good example of this kind of trip is from Algonquin Park in Ontario to Huntsville, on Highway 60, about a fifty-mile trip with a great variety of water and interest. Many trips of this kind may be planned with comparable proximity to railroads, because local trains generally can be flagged down in Canada at off-station points, not only in emergencies but also for canoeists whose trips start on rivers or lakes that cross or parallel railroad rights-of-way.

Starting canoe trips that depart directly from auto roads or railroads is also valuable for the matured canoe voyager, because it generally gives him the advantage of getting into the wilderness area without preliminary travel through semipopulated regions. Numerous rivers crossed by the Alcan Highway place the canoe voyager in the wilderness in the first hour. The most northerly railroads, such as the route to Churchill on Hudson Bay, offer this same accessibility. Surveys are being made for a railroad from the Hay River to Great Slave Lake in the Northwest Territories, opening still another front of embarkation points.

It is now possible for canoe trips to reach even the arctic tundra without extensive access canoe travel, by

Chartered Flights . . . Should Be Cleared

departing from the Alcan Highway, from the Hudson Bay Railroad, from scheduled coastal boats, and especially from seaplane ports with scheduled flights.

In the use of planes, there will likely be the problem of obtaining a canoe at the airport point of canoe embarkation, although canoes can be made available in many instances if one plans far enough in advance. Chartered flights on which canoes are to be taken should be cleared in advance with airline's dispatchers or with individual fliers, because many airway companies or individuals will not carry large canoes on the undercarriage where canoes are apt to change the aerodynamic operation of the plane.

A good plan is to ship your own canoe far in advance to

the most remote transit embarkation point—by railroad freight, steamer, truck, and in some areas in winter by caterpillar train or snowmobile.

Satisfactory sectional canoes, which can be bolted together, are made for airplane transportation, and are accepted in chartered flights because they can be carried inside the plane. The Hudson's Bay Company moves freight to outposts for their own use, and may welcome your outfit if it is moved in keeping with their own scheduled boat or flight loads. The Hudson's Bay Company has just recently inaugurated what they call their U-Paddle Canoe Rental Service; 17-foot aluminum canoes are stationed at various points throughout the Canadian North, including Yellowknife, Waterways, Île à la Crosse, La Ronge, Norway House, and Winnipeg. Letters of inquiry should be addressed to the Outpost Division, Hudson's Bay House, Winnipeg, Manitoba, Canada. (Also see chapter 11.)

Canadian railroads are exceptionally accommodating when it comes to embarkation points. Local trains will generally stop at trestles, or outlying waterfronts, where there is neither station nor settlement, and you can return from that point by flagging the local train on your return. Some of the smaller steamers will also let you off at remote points, putting your canoe in the water, and allowing you to paddle ashore. Sometimes the sea is too heavy for such departure from a steamer, but wilderness port ships— when not of great tonnage—will usually let you off in the lee of some headland, where you can get ashore and wait in a camp for quieter water. Later you can skirt the coast by canoe, and reach your embarkation point at the mouth of a river or inlet.

Any trip of significance in a wilderness area may wisely

be planned a year, or at least several months, ahead. Where freight is moved by steamer only once a year to outposts in the Far North, the importance of a long *time* element in plans is obvious. Advance planning is also wise even when guides are to be employed.

If you do not use guides on major canoe trips, be sure that your own experience is ample. If you use guides, employ only those based on responsible recommendation. Guides are sometimes inexperienced individuals who are looking for a short period of employment, or they are would-be guides. I have used such people, but only because for a particular route I was looking for strong backs. It may be well to have an understanding before you start, if your own decisions in conducting the voyage are to be the final decisions. But when you employ an experienced guide, on whom you intend to rely for your safety and the success of the voyage, his judgment should be given high respect.

Those individuals with limited experience who may question the cost or the merit of guides should remember that high-class guides are not employed only to expedite the trip. A competent guide will impart a treasure of wilderness craft to you that is a permanent addition to your fund of knowledge. Watch your guide work. If he is competent, your whole trip will be one of hourly revelation. If you treat him as though he were a servant, the chances are that you will get little more for your money than a politely conducted, safe voyage. If you regard him as a fellow voyager, and shoulder your part of the load, he is quite sure to open up around the campfire with a wealth of information—trail romance that will make the trip memorable.

When you read the chapter on Canoe Voyage Equipment and Its Use, be sure that you make your selections for the season of the year and overlapping seasons in a particular area or areas in which you are to travel, whether forest, tundra, mountain, or prairie. Also, consider that you may travel from one of these regions to another, requiring food and equipment for the various regions and also for a wide variation in seasonal temperature. For example, on mountain rivers, you may need tracking lines several hundred feet long, where in another region, hundred-foot lines may suffice. On the tundra, where the only available fuel may be nothing more than some dry heather, or none at all, you need a primus or other gas stove for cooking. In the western part of the Northwest Territories of Canada, where rapids may be given a comparative index rating of "dangerous," it is wise to consider large canoes, not less than 18 feet in length—preferably 20 feet, in some instances—and of fairly wide beam. Also, check the adequacy of your clothing for the seasonal overlap.

Canoes shipped by freight to arrive long in advance of a trip must be covered with a buffer padding of burlap and straw. Two layers of burlap with straw sewn between, using a large needle, can be patterned to fit the canoe and readily tied into place. Canoes can be shipped by express, or as baggage unprotected, but the rate is considerably higher than that for wrapped canoes and about four times higher than equal weight in more compact pieces of baggage. Paddles and the portaging yoke should be securely tied inside the gunwales for shipment, never packed separately.

Where canoes are hauled on car tops, the carriers need to be insulated with rubber to avoid wearing grooves into the canoe's gunwales. This can be done by slipping automobile radiator hose over the crossbars of the car-top carriers. Such pieces of hose should be big enough in diameter to roll loosely on the cross members. This greatly facilitates your loading of the canoe by yourself because it can be rolled into place after one end is lifted onto one of the carriers, and likewise rolled off.

Equipment and provisions for shipment by rail, ship, plane or truck are best packed in easily opened, hinged-cover, wooden shipping cases, or foot lockers—never in exposed packsacks. Packsacks will get dragged over dirty, oily, wood-splintered, baggage-house floors, and suffer considerable damage. If you must ship the packsacks themselves tie them, or better, sew them into burlap covers.

When crossing international borders, you must submit to inspection by customs and interrogation by immigration. Between Canada and the United States, the coming and going is a comparatively simple process. The agents on both sides are generally very helpful and considerate of your pleasure and welfare. Camp equipment is usually passed over the border without question. Outboard motors should be well drained, then boxed, with the year, serial number, and the new or old retail value marked on the outside of the packing case for customs' records. A too generous supply of alcoholic liquors and tobacco may be questioned. If you carry more than a few days' supply of food, duty may be imposed. There is no point in provisioning in one country and crossing a boundary with such food supplies unless you are certain that the particular foods you desire are not available in the other country. These may, of course, be certain dehydrated, freeze-dried foods, or special diet foods. Recent legislation in Canada compels all canoeists to include life preservers and an extra paddle. Carry identification that will, if necessary, establish your citizenship.

4 THE CANOEIST'S ART

PART ONE

OVER the past two decades there has been enough controversy over canoe strokes and general handling of the canoe to warrant comparison of new procedures with the old. Since canoe travel has had a great historical era, this may seem presumptuous. But technical analysis of all mental, manual, and mechanical functions in recent years has enabled us to run faster, pole-vault higher, and has generally improved the dexterity of man in relation to his increasing facilities.

While a number of changes have taken place in the canoeist's art, the two most conspicuous advances are the revised methods for maintaining a true, forward course of the canoe, without obvious steering, and the improved procedure for running rapids.

It must be understood that the widest part of the canoe (the center), because it is most buoyant, is the pivot point on which the canoe swings from side to side, and the fulcrum on which the bow and stern move or teeter up and down.

When two paddlers, one in the bow, the other in the stern, make equal, simple strokes for moving the canoe forward, the canoe veers to the opposite side from which

the stern paddler is working. The reason for this, mathe-
matically, is that the stern paddler's leverage position,
compared to the bow paddler's leverage position, is greater
in direct ratio to the central pivot point of the canoe.

The tendency for the canoe to veer from its forward
course may be partially offset by putting the stronger
paddler in the bow. Generally, however, this is not sufficient compensation against the veering tendency. And
since the stronger paddler is usually a larger individual,
his additional weight throws the canoe out of balance,
creating a further steering problem, for a canoe is best
maneuvered when the bow is slightly higher in the water
than the stern. But only *slightly*.

To maintain a straight course, the common practice
over the years has been for the stern paddler to give a
slight outward rudder thrust with his paddle at the end
of each stroke. This in common canoe vernacular is called
a "J" stroke, since the complete motion of the stroke
describes the letter J. But whenever a paddle is used in
this outward fashion, it impedes the forward progress of
the canoe. A few ounces of energy exerted on each outward rudder thrust, multiplied by the thousands of strokes
in a day of paddling, runs into tons of wasted energy
and, at the same time, becomes equivalent to several lost
miles.

Some canoe instructors propose that the way to overcome the veering is to "knife" the paddle out of the water.
I have tested this method, and found that it uses up even
more energy than the outward thrust operation. Both are
inefficient. Working on the theory that the forward directional control of the canoe could largely be handled by a
straight-back stroke, I have sought to refine the forward

impelling stroke until it lost most of the inefficiency caused by the commonly practiced, added steering operation. The result is what I have termed the *pitch stroke*.

Objections may be made that the stroke is conventional and not a further development. To the nontechnical eye there may be no significant distinction between the pitch stroke and the conventional stroke. The main difference lies in two factors. First, those who practice the conventional stroke "knife" the blade out of the water at the last part of the stroke to complete the steering, and continue this knifing to the surface of the water. At the last part of the stroke there is a water lift that uses up as much energy as the entire pitch stroke, thus doubling the energy in the conventional stroke to accomplish the same forward motion achieved by the pitch stroke. Secondly, in the knifing operation the paddle must of necessity be brought to the surface to complete the stroke, which defeats the deep-water use of the paddle for a quick change of pace to another stroke such as the sculling draw. The pitch stroke is completed deep in the water where the paddle is ready for the sculling draw. It comes to the surface only after the stroke is completed, and without use of energy.

The pitch stroke is performed in the following manner:

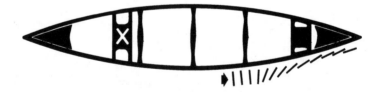

Pitch Stroke

The paddle is started in the usual fashion, the flat surface of the vertical blade held at right angles to the side of the canoe. As the blade is brought back against the water, the inside edge of the blade is gradually turned toward the stern of the canoe, and continues to turn until, at the end of the stroke, the surface of the blade is parallel to the side of the canoe, but still *deep in the water*. The paddle is then brought out of the water edgewise—with no resistance whatever to the water—and the stroke is repeated. In fact, the paddle actually floats to the surface at the end of the stroke, and is not knifed out at an angle as in the conventional performance of this type of stroke. Thus, the canoe is propelled on a straightforward course with a canoe stroke that is directly back, in no way impeding the forward motion of the canoe. The stroke is most efficient when the paddle is used as close to the canoe as possible without touching it.

Some modification can be practiced in the pitch stroke, if preferred, by bringing the paddle back as described, but instead of turning the paddle until it is parallel to the side of the canoe, the paddle can remain at a pitch angle through the stroke, and when still deep in the water, slipped out of the water edgewise toward the side for the next stroke.

The difficulty with this stroke, at first, is that, while grasping the paddle in the conventional manner, the paddler finds it hard to turn the blade surface from the right-angle position at the start of the stroke to the parallel position at the end of the stroke. But this difficulty can be overcome by grasping the knob of the paddle backhanded, instead of at the usual front position. A few strokes in this backhand manner should be practiced, and soon the paddler will be able to modify the grip into a position best suited for manipulating the paddle. But it should never be grasped in front, as is commonly done.

The point at which the stern paddler in the pitch stroke begins to turn his paddle and the degree of angle it is to be turned are determined entirely by the compensating strength of the bow paddler's stroke against that of the stern paddler. Sometimes the pitch of the stern paddle must be extreme, and begin almost at the start of the stroke. Sometimes it may not have to start sooner than two-thirds of the way back, to compensate for the veering tendency of the canoe and to keep it going on a straightforward course. (See diagram of *pitch stroke*. Note carefully not only the position of the paddle blade relative to the canoe at all parts of the stroke, but also the general direction of the blade throughout the course of the stroke.) Above all, bear in mind that the force of the stroke ends deep in the water—not at the surface, as in the more common methods, and that the paddle, when brought out of the water for the next stroke, merely floats out, or is brought out edgewise without resistance.

The next important stroke is one used in the new method of running rapids, and in all side or lateral movement of the canoe.

The early way of running rapids was to get the canoe going faster than the flow of the current, to be able to steer with the paddle as a rudder, and to make more effective additional steerage with a quarter-sweep of the paddle. A canoe drifting rapidly down through the rapids cannot be controlled simply by using the paddle as a fixed rudder. Canoe and paddle would merely float helter-skelter along with the current, and have no rudder resistance to the water at all. When the canoe is speeded up by energetic paddling, and goes faster than the current, the rudder effect is immediately felt.

However, it is easy to see that as the speed of the canoe in rapids increases, the hazards also increase. If the canoe could, therefore, be allowed to drift through the rapids, keeping its direction and lateral maneuverability for position in white-water channels, the trip would be much safer, and more equipment could be taken downriver without having to be portaged.

The solution, then, to the problem of directional and lateral control of the canoe floating through the rapids is a stroke which will draw either the bow or the stern strongly from one side to the other; or if need be, cause the entire canoe to slip sidewise (laterally) to bring it into a proper channel. This stroke is called the *sculling draw*. The stroke may be best described by the diagram. Observe carefully the general direction of the blade of the paddle and the position of the paddle at all times during this movement. Thus the stroke may be readily understood.

The paddle is held at an *angle* from point *A* to *B*, in the manner of a propeller blade. Then the paddle is drawn *flat* against the water from *B* to *C*. At *C* the paddle is again turned at propeller-blade angle, and moved from *C* to *D*. Then, again, the paddle is drawn *flat* against the water from *D* back to *A*, at which point the entire stroke is repeated. With the sculling draw, backwater strokes can be taken at intervals, if necessary in running rapids to slow down the canoe; also, if needed, a severe quarter-sweep stroke can be applied to effect a quick turn. (See *quarter-sweep stroke*.)

When the bow paddler works on the right side of the canoe, the stern paddler on the left, the sculling draw

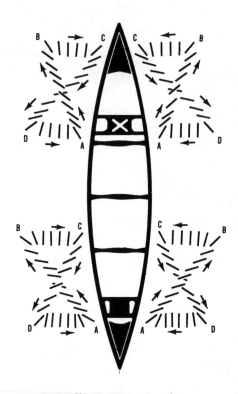

Sculling Draw Stroke

stroke turns the canoe to the right. And, of course, if the positions are reversed, the canoe turns to the left. If both paddlers work on the same side, the entire canoe will slip laterally toward the side on which the paddlers are working. The bow paddler should call the signals for avoiding rock obstacles and the proper channeling of the canoe, because he has the best view of obstacles and free channels. The sculling draw stroke is sometimes referred to as the *figure 8 stroke*, but I think the whole stroke best describes the shape of an hourglass, or the letter *x*. The stroke has not reached its maximum efficiency unless there is a strong, continuous, lateral pull to the paddle through-out the stroke.

It is absolutely essential that the paddler assume a kneel-ing position when running rapids, whether or not the sculling draw stroke is used. The most stable position is to kneel on both knees, spreading them as far apart as possible into the bilges of the canoe, and resting your buttocks against the canoe seat. In fact, it might be re-garded as partial sitting on the rear seat and partial kneel-ing. This supporting position prevents the paddler from being thrown backward, while his knees prevent him from pitching forward. His wide knee stance keeps him from being thrown to the right or left. The position offers strong leverage on the paddle for all maneuvers. Thus, as an equestrian rides *with* his horse, you ride *with* your canoe.

The *quarter-sweep stroke* is occasionally used as an aux-iliary stroke to the sculling draw; it helps to swing the bow or stern from side to side. This stroke is executed by placing the paddle forward and flat against the canoe at the bow and sweeping outward—close to the surface of the water—until the paddle is extended at right angles to the canoe. In the stern the paddle is placed back and parallel with the canoe, sweeping out until it too is at right angles to the canoe. To turn the canoe quickly with the quarter-sweep, the strokes are made simultaneously by the bow and stern paddlers, working, of course, on op-posite sides.

When a paddler is alone in a canoe in rough water, where he must work from the center of the canoe approx-imately midway between bow and stern but slightly back, he uses the *full sweep stroke*, instead of the quarter-sweep,

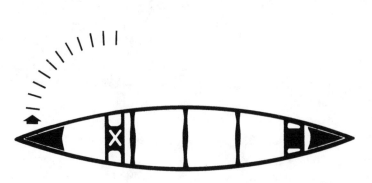

Quarter-Sweep Stroke

to make a rapid turn. The paddle is placed forward and parallel to the canoe, and is swept close to the surface all the way back until it is again parallel to the canoe. This stroke turns him toward the opposite side from which he is paddling. The regular stroke for forward motion when paddling alone is the pitch stroke.

The *bow rudder* is seldom used. It is merely extending the paddle forward at the bow as a rudder to avoid hitting a deadhead or other obstruction. Either the sculling draw or the quarter-sweep is generally more effective in this instance.

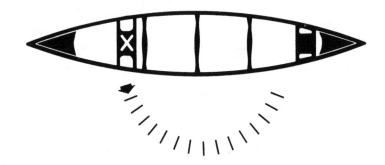

Full Sweep Stroke

The *J stroke*, referred to earlier, is a novice's stern paddling stroke. The paddle blade is brought back through the water at right angles to the canoe, and then at the end of the stroke is either thrust out slightly as a rudder or, as described, knifed out of the water for canoe control. It is inefficient, and should be largely eliminated from the canoeist's art in favor of the pitch stroke. Its value is as a temporary trial-and-error stroke for the beginner.

The *diagonal draw stroke*, an all-around paddling stroke, is simple in theory but difficult to execute. Its advantage is that the blade is always brought flat against the water, the various angles of draw being used to control direction without apparent steering. It is a plain case of drawing the bow or stern, with simple paddle strokes, in whatever direction you want the bow or stern to go— forward, sidewise, backward, or in between. The difficult part of the stroke is that it is worthless unless bow and stern paddlers operate as a well-coordinated team. Once

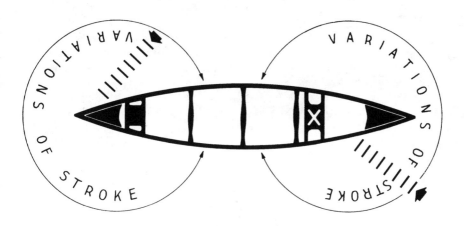

Diagonal Draw Stroke

Underwater Stroke

the coordination of paddlers is perfected, it is a valuable stroke for use in heavy seas, especially with or against heavy winds, and competitive racing. The illustration shows it applied to one angle; the curved arrows show the variety of angles to which it can be applied. Imagine the paddler's position as the hub of a wagon wheel lying flat, with the spokes describing the various strokes. Thus, the strokes start at the rim of the wheel, and are drawn toward the hub—the paddler.

The *underwater stroke* is used for approaching wary wildlife, and must be executed soundlessly. It is the same as the pitch stroke, except that the paddle is not brought out of the water at the end of the stroke. To do it silently, revolve the paddle completely on each stroke, as shown in the diagram. Here again, note carefully not only the direction of the paddle, but the angle of the blade at all parts of the stroke, and that the paddle remains fully submerged both when beginning and repeating the stroke.

PART TWO

With a knowledge of canoe strokes, we can now proceed to simulate part of a canoe voyage to see how the methods and strokes apply, and to consider a few concepts of general canoe travel.

An empty canoe seems very unstable and "tippy" to the individual unacquainted with its physical nature. One has the same sensation the first time in a saddle on a spirited mount. A canoe with a load of camping equipment in it, on the other hand, seems very stable. This is because the center of gravity has been lowered and greatly counterbalanced. To illustrate the principle, float a drinking glass in water. It has a tendency to tip over and sink. But with a silver dollar or two flat in the bottom of the glass, it will be stable and have no tendency to upset.

If this principle of low gravity is kept in mind for the canoe, and all actions are balanced in the center from side to side, most of the upset risk is eliminated. As you are kicked around in a heavy sea or rapids, think of the cowboy who rides the Brahma bulls: Nothing serious happens, no matter how rough the ride, until he gets off center. As mentioned earlier, you must assume a kneeling position at all times in rough seas and rapids.

A canoe may become windbound when the sea is running at right angles to its direction of travel. But, surprisingly perhaps, a canoe will ride parallel with unusually high waves and will not swamp if, by your secure kneeling position, you can maintain the the touchy balance of the cowboy on the Brahma bull. Upsets in a canoe on a heavy sea are rarely caused by wash of big waves into a canoe, but rather by a paddler getting off balance and "not riding with his mount." Good sense demands, of course, that when there is no need for risks, you simply should not take them.

When you are compelled to cross a heavy sea running at right angles to your direction of travel, it can be done by tacking. Turn the bow of your canoe into the wind, then swing the bow about ten degrees off from windward in the direction you want to go, and hold this position with diagonal draw strokes, or the pitch stroke.

The wave action against the side of your canoe will tack the canoe laterally toward your goal. All that is necessary is enough paddle action to keep the canoe in this position and to prevent it from drifting backward. However, by using the diagonal draw, or a sculling draw, this sidewise direction can be speeded up. By being thus headed into the wind and waves, the risk of swamping is at a minimum.

Frequently, a voyage is made with more than one canoe. Most any sea, no matter how rough, can be run if two canoes are lashed together in catamaran fashion. Use two *green-cut* poles for strength and flexibility. Lash the poles to the front and stern thwarts, using your tracking lines, so that the bows of the canoes are 4 feet apart, the sterns 6 feet apart. The difference in spacing prevents the water from piling up between the canoes and washing over the gunwales. This same spacing method must be employed when using motor power even in calm water to avoid the pileup of water between the canoes.

An improvised sail can be used with great safety in this catamaran way. Mount the tent ground sheet with poles at the bow for the sail, and steer with paddles at the stern. By laying planks across two canoes, heavy items, such as stoves, bottle-gas refrigerators, and other items used in cabins in the wilderness can be transported. (For a comprehensive treatment of this subject, see my book, *The Wilderness Cabin*, published by The Macmillan Company.)

When traveling through a heavy running sea in a single canoe, it is wise to employ a sea anchor, especially when you start out on a big area of water with an offshore wind. As you get miles out into the sea, the waves become increasingly higher, and if they become so bad that there is danger the canoe will become awash, you may have to start bailing. The bow man ordinarily does this, but the sea may become so rough that one man's paddling is not sufficient. You will then have to resort to a sea anchor. For a canoe, the best anchor is your largest cooking pail tied to a rope—tied with a secure knot. You should provide for this emergency by preparing the sea anchor before embarking.

Use enough rope so that it can be run through both sides of the back seat supports and around both sides of the canoe to the keel, where it is knotted. And from this knot at the keel, the rope should extend about fifteen feet to the cooking pail. The lashing you made around the seat to the keel is called a "bridle," in canoe terminology. The pail is set inside the canoe, the fifteen feet of rope coiled up beside it.

When the sea begins to roll too heavily, throw the pail out into the water behind the canoe. As the rope tightens from the forward motion of the canoe, the pail will start filling with water, and will sink just below the surface. The wind may have been tearing away at your canoe, driving you along, threatening a broadside to the waves, but once the rope has tightened, it performs two functions: It keeps your stern headed into the running sea so that your canoe cannot get broadside of the waves; and as it pulls from the keel, it helps to keep your canoe upright and stable. Both paddlers should get down on the floor of the canoe to lower the center of gravity for additional safety. As water comes in, keep bailing with a pail, can, hat, or even your cupped hands. As you near the far shore, be prepared to leap out and save the canoe from being wrecked on the rocks or shore debris. If all of your equipment is packed, as I have suggested, in waterproof containers, it is wise to upset the canoe just before you reach shore to slow it down. First rescue the empty canoe; the rest will float ashore if it is properly packed.

A further point about the bridle: Whenever you are towing one or more canoes by a motorized canoe, be sure to prepare the same bridle arrangement on the stern of the towing canoe and on the bow of the towed canoe. This draws the towed canoe up over the water and prevents it from bobbing around in off-course curves, and keeps the bow from plowing water. The bridle will keep the canoe in a straight line, riding high on the water—providing you have loaded any equipment in the towed canoe slightly back.

When your course is heading directly into the wind, the canoe's veering tendency may be offset by swinging the bow offwind just a few degrees toward the side on which the stern paddler is working. This will enable him to eliminate most of the pitch angle for steering in his stroke, and thus to use the energy entirely for forward motion. You need all the energy you have in a heavy head wind. And the slight zigzag course necessitated by this process is a small sacrifice for the greater gain of simpler canoe control.

When paddling a canoe alone, the position taken in a wind is at the center—the widest part of the canoe—just back of the center thwart, or yoke. The canoe, of course, can be ballasted at the bow, and the kneeling position assumed at the stern. When paddling in the center, heading into the wind, the paddler will have to crowd the center thwart, knees under the thwart, the arms and body extended forward as much as possible. When running with the wind, the paddling position assumed is just back from the center thwart. The reason for this is that the canoe acts like a weather vane, and if one end is high, it will swing downwind. Obviously, if various maneuvers are to be made, the body position has to be shifted back and forth, toward and away from the center thwart as needed. Thus you have the wind, which otherwise works against you, doing part of the work.

In my early days of canoe travel, canoe keels were great subjects of controversy—arguments around campfires lasted far into the night. For the expert canoeist, the canoe without a keel is the most responsive to maneuver. The standard keel is a strip of material extending out about three-quarters of an inch along the center of the bottom of the canoe, its chief purpose being to protect the bottom from rocks and other obstructions. It helps to stabilize the upright position of a canoe; but it also stabilizes the straightforward motion of the canoe, which can be a disadvantage in running rapids, where quick turns are essential. Canoes can be specially equipped with shoe keels, which protect the bottom without interfering very much with fast turning. A shoe keel is a strip of material lying flat along the center line of the bottom of the canoe; on wood and canvas canoes, the strip is about an inch and a half wide and three-eighths of an inch thick. Aluminum canoes need standard keels to support the floor and for protection against rocks and other hazards.

Generally, the expressed disadvantages of a keel, while technically real, are overemphasized. A canoe that does a great deal of wilderness service should have a keel of some kind for protection.

Paddle length can also become controversial. Try various lengths—from just under your chin up to the level of your eyes, when the blade rests vertically at your feet. You will arrive at a length between those two points which suits you best.

PART THREE

Let us assume that you have shipped your canoe and equipment to an embarkation point in the wilderness. A small freighter has put you ashore behind a sheltering headland, and you have reached the mouth of a great wilderness river for an extensive canoe voyage inland. The river and the sea have formed a long, rough-water inlet. For additional safety you load the canoe as near the center as possible, but with the bow slightly lighter than the stern. Center loading gives the bow and stern more buoyancy, and consequently lessens the chance of shipping water as the canoe pitches through the whitecapped waves of the inlet. This advantage becomes evident when you are under way—the bow plunging down suddenly, with terrific impact, while the stern seems almost to be sucked under with each receding wave. Your load should also be in perfect balance from side to side—what we call "well trimmed."

At the far end of the inlet where it merges with the river, you discover the current to be quite fast, but perhaps not creating rapids, as it makes its last descent to the ocean level. After a while in this fast water, you become aware that paddling has been heavy—with scarcely any forward progress against the racing water. If the shore will permit some sort of travel afoot, no matter how rough, it is best to land, attach lines, and tow the loaded canoe against the current—known as "tracking" or "lining."

Tracking the Canoe

In tracking or lining the canoe upstream, the stern line is attached to the rear seat, the bowline to the towing link at the extreme front end of the canoe. If the river has so many obstructions that the canoe will frequently founder, one man will have to paddle and guide it while the other does the towing, handling both lines alone. In a river fairly free of obstructions, both men tow. Always keep a firm hold on towing lines, and use secure knots to attach the lines to the canoe; the power of moving water is unbelievable. (See illustration of bowline knot.) The common practice of tying towlines is in reverse of the method described above. Most of the time, this arrangement works quite well, but in very rough water it becomes a risk. A rope from the front seat allows more current wash against the bow than sometimes can be controlled, especially if the bow towman momentarily loses too much tension on his line.

To start towing the canoe upstream, force the bow

gently out into the stream, holding the stern line taut. The wash of the current on the near side of the bow will make the canoe tack out into the water. As soon as the canoe is awash by the current on the near side of the bow and begins to move out into the stream, the bowline is also brought up taut, and both men start towing upstream. The canoe is in a good towing position when there is a slight constant wash (tack) of the current on the near side of the bow—this towing position or angle of the current being regulated by pulling harder on one line or the other.

Rapids that allow a canoe to be towed upstream can often, but not always, be run downstream with paddles. If there is a chance to track or line a canoe downstream, where poling or running rapids with a paddle might incur a greater risk, it is certainly wiser to track. (Tracking or lining a canoe downstream is having the canoe drift downstream, controlled by lines.) The downstream process is similar to tracking upstream, except that in the downstream control of the canoe, the tack is against the near side of the *stern*. In downstream tracking, the canoe is being held back by the trackers, checked just enough to keep the current going a little faster than the canoe speed, in order to maintain this tack against the near side of the stern. In downstream tracking, remember that the front line should be fastened to the front seat, the rear line to the rear "towing" link. If the water is very rough, do not risk switching these positions of the lines on the canoe.

In downstream tracking or lining, it is most important to see that the *stern* of the canoe does not swing out of control; in upstream tracking see that the *bow* does not swing out of control. A good way to remember this is that the line fastened to the towing link is always on the end of the canoe headed into the current. If the stern gets away in downstream tracking, or the bow gets away in upstream tracking, there is apt to be a broadside of the canoe to the current, causing a heavy wash and roll that may cause an upset. This can scarcely happen with the ropes tied on the canoe in the positions suggested, the lines held firm, and the footing watched carefully at every step.

If one end of the canoe does accidentally swing out of control, don't fight it, but let the uncontrolled end drift around parallel with the current, by releasing one line. When possible, hold onto the line fastened to the towing link. Recover the canoe to shore, drain it if it has shipped water, and start over.

You can be generous in the length of your tracking lines, as they extend not only out into the current, but also downstream, and at times, into a canyon, to a considerable depth where cataracts tumble through rocky fissures. For most of my canoe travel I have found that two lines, each 150 feet long, of new No. 5 or 6 cotton sash cord, treated with a solution of turpentine 2 quarts, beeswax 8 ounces, and oil of tar ½ ounce, are satisfactory. Melt the beeswax, pour it into the turpentine and tar oil mixture, and dip the rope, then drain it in the hot sun. I do not like the synthetic fiber ropes because they present problems in knot tying and other rope handling. Attach lines to the canoe with a bowline knot for ease of untying.

An important advantage gained in all tracking is that the canoe load is reduced by the weight of both paddlers.

Sometimes rivers are shallow enough to warrant walking through the current and pushing the canoe upstream through the fast stretches of water. Protective footwear is, of course, needed.

Poling the Canoe

If the water is too deep for wading and pushing the canoe, it can sometimes be poled upstream. Each man uses a slender pole about 12 feet long, cut from the shoreline forest. If much poling is done, sometimes a soft, cuplike iron shoe (which any machine shop can supply) is slipped over the end of the pole that enters the water, and is held there by a single nail through a hole in the side of the shoe. (To remove the shoe, burn it off in a campfire.) The weight of the iron shoe helps to keep the pole down in the water, and prevents it from "brooming." The pole should be reduced in size where the shoe goes on to prevent it from catching between the rocks. The iron shoe is not essential, however, and I find it practical to trim off the brooming end with an ax periodically, if the pole is used continually.

The polers stand or kneel in the canoe, and, while snubbing the end of the pole on the river bottom, push the canoe upriver, or fend it from the rocks when going downstream where paddling is not feasible.

Once the poles are snubbed on the bottom, it is a hand-over-hand process until the end of the pole is reached; then the pole is reset in an advance position, and the process repeated. Whether you work the poles alternately or simultaneously will depend on the immediate angle of the canoe in relation to the direction of the current. Most often, both polers work on one side of the canoe. It is a tricky business, calling for balance and quick reactions. One common cause of failure is the tendency to support the pole with only one hand at a time. Both hands should be used to give spring to the pole, thus drawing the bow or stern from side to side by the pole bending tension, as well as forward.

I know of no part of the canoeist's art that is based so much on experience rather than theory as poling a canoe. Some canoe men have very orthodox notions about poling. Listen receptively; then get your own experience —a lot of it. Try working in shallow rapids until you catch on to it.

Poling can be done downstream if the rapids are not too strong, but it is not satisfactory unless the rapids are moderate. Most deep rapids can be run, using paddles. In shallow rapids, poles should be used to guide the canoe downstream, in and out of rocks. Never use paddles for poling; they break easily, or their ends may broom out, becoming heavy and soggy. Where the rapids are more than shallow but still moderate, the poles can be snubbed down heavily along the bottom as a brake, and alternately used forward against the rocks for a smooth descent.

Fast water and even rapids can sometimes be ascended with an outboard motor. A combination of pole or paddles and outboard motor is sometimes possible, if the water is deep enough to keep the prop running free, or if the motor is jet-impelled, with no propeller. The jet motor does not extend below the keel line, and is therefore a valuable propulsion unit for running or descending rapids, as it generally clears any obstructions that have already been cleared by the canoe itself.

Where it is possible to ascend a stretch of rapids or fast water with a motorized canoe, the motor should be fixed in a straightforward position by tightening the steering bearing clamp. The canoe is then controlled with paddles —using the sculling-draw and quarter-sweep stroke—or poles. When descending rapids with a motorized canoe, fix the motor in reverse, again tightening the steering bearing clamp, and keep the motor running only fast enough to hold the canoe back for a moderate drift downstream, doing all steering with poles or paddles.

Portaging

There are some rapids you can neither pole, nor track, nor run with a motor. There are cataracts too violent and cascades too steep to ascend or descend. These must be portaged.

The side of the river on which the portage trail is located is often indicated on your map, or it may be appar-

Portaging the Canoe

ent by the contour of the approach. Snub the canoe up to the bank with both bow and stern lines before unloading. Immediately after unloading, remove the canoe from the water to drain and to prevent its being damaged against the rocks.

The best approach to portage trails in a strange country is to carry the packs over first to avoid having to seek out

Keep the Camera Ready

the trail with the canoe overhead, limiting your vision.

If all the equipment has been properly consolidated into the main packs, there will be no loose items to get lost. (See Chapter 13 for packing methods. For a comprehensive, detailed coverage of all forms of camp equipment and procedure, see my book, *The New Way of the Wilderness*, The Macmillan Company.)

A ready camera should be on the person of at least one member of the party at all times—on trail or water—preferably the man ahead, and if the camera is not equipped with an automatic diaphragm, it should be continually reset manually for the existing light condition. There may be ample time to set the shutter, or even to make exposure meter readings of the light conditions, but when you suddenly come upon wildlife, and delay, the fleeting picture is likely to be gone forever. If, however, the focus is set at an emergency distance of about 18 to 25 feet, using as small a diaphragm opening as possible in relation to a shutter speed for a hand-held exposure, pictures at almost any average distance will be fairly passable. Of course, if time permits, you should adjust the distance, lens opening and shutter speed for the exact conditions required for each exposure.

Your canoe must be equipped with a portaging yoke, either one that replaces the center thwart or the channeled type fitting over the center thwart for added support. The factory-made yoke, with an aluminum crossbar and two cushion pads, is a poorly adapted piece of equipment that bears down painfully on the deltoid muscles. If you pride yourself as a canoe voyager, remove the pads and attach a plastic molded yoke made by Fiberglas canoe manufacturers, or make your own yoke in the pioneer pattern for carrying two buckets of water—the type that covers the entire upper part of the back and shoulders. The yoke should be of light wood—preferably white spruce or cottonwood with a good grain—and carved by hand with chisels, gouges, and rasps, then finished with sandpaper and waterproofed with a liquid floor sealer or aluminum enamel. I built mine from thin, laminated pieces of glued wood in order to get good strength. Sponge rubber cemented to the yoke for padding is a mess in the rain, and if the yoke fits the shoulders well, no cushioning is necessary. If you do use a sponge rubber pad, tie it on, so that it can be removed and wrung out. To make a yoke pattern, stand in the position assumed when portaging the canoe. Have someone grease your shoulders over the area which the yoke will cover, and then apply plaster of Paris, which

will set in a few minutes. Make a wooden yoke to con-
form generally, not in detail, to the plaster pattern. Remove the pads from the aluminum crossbar of the factory-
made yoke, then attach your wooden shoulder form to
the crossbar, using screws.

A canoe is generally picked up by one man; but if your
partner will lift one end and allow you to walk under it
into position at the portaging yoke, it will be a lot easier.

To pick up a canoe without help, stand at the yoke to
one side of the upright canoe. Roll the canoe away from
you, onto its side. Place your knee against the bottom of
the canoe, and roll the canoe, balanced from end to end,
toward you up on your knee. Then grasp the gunwales—
your left hand in front of the yoke, your right hand behind it—and with an additional boost from your knee, lift
the canoe to your shoulders. Reverse this procedure at the
other end of the portage.

If the portage is a long one, you can rest from time to
time by wedging the bow in the branches or crotch of a
tree. This way you don't have to ground the canoe and
again lift it to your shoulders. On long portages you can
alternate with your partner from canoe to packs.

Once you are over the portage trail, you can gain an
advantage by embarking systematically. To launch the
canoe, set it upright on the ground, and with one man on
each side of the center, simultaneously pick up the canoe
by the gunwales, and feed it, stern first, into the water
when going upstream—bow first for downstream. The
reason for this will at once become apparent. When going
upstream, the stern will drift downstream as you hang
onto the bow; when going downstream, the bow will
drift downstream as you hang onto the stern. It simply
launches the canoe in the direction you wish to go. When

launching the canoe on a lakeshore beach, feed it in stern first; then as the stern paddler's weight is applied to the end position of the stern seat, the bow is consequently lifted and lightened for take-off.

These constant little applications of improved method make the difference between smooth action and uncomfortable struggle.

Until now, the pressures and excitement of fast-water canoe travel have dominated your course—a succession of adventures which have not been the wilderness solitude you had envisioned. But finally, beyond the rapids, you discover that the river has lost most of its fury, flowing around curve after curve, past little green islands that look like green-masted ships slowly heading for the sea. You hear only the rhythmic dip of your paddle in this imposing hush. An occasional bad stroke bangs the paddle against the canoe, and you are shocked—and embarrassed —at breaking the silence. *This* is the solitude you dreamed about.

Around curve and placid expanse, the silence seems to grow deeper, then suddenly two mallards sweep by overhead, apparently frightened by some large animal you hear crashing noisily back in the forest. The river begins to expand. Wild rice beds loom up, and almost magically replace the rockbound shores. When you pull up to the shore to examine the unfolding scene, you notice deep moose tracks, the mud and water just settling back into each fresh pocket.

The rewards of portage and paddle are beginning to pay off. But the swish of your paddle strokes and your excited voices have become startling warnings to the wildlife across the overflow and ahead on the river. Flocks of

The Rewards of Portage and Paddle Are Beginning to Pay Off

wild fowl have been rising and milling over forest and lowland, coming to rest only after they have surveyed the possible hazard of your presence, and then settling in remote bays of the marsh. You realize that you must now alter your paddling tactics, and abandon the pitch stroke for the silent underwater stroke, one that will permit stalking your way upriver with absolute quiet.

As you settle into the smooth, quiet rhythm of this stroke, you dare not even whisper. To call your partner's attention to a caribou camouflaged against a rocky background beyond the point, or a flock of young merganser ducks hugging the shore current, you rock the canoe gently. A short while back, you altered your conduct for wilderness society. In time, the orderly, respectful protocol of the wilderness will come as naturally as breathing, and only then will you be accepted into the silent forest mansions.

Hour after hour, a hush dominates the river's course, but eventually it is broken. For the last few minutes you have been conscious of a strange murmuring sound. You wonder if it is the blood pulsing in your ears. Suddenly, the air becomes cool and humid; the river's current quickens slightly. Innumerable patches of foam appear on the water, and as canyon walls loom into view, you discover the reasons for the noise and atmospheric change—a waterfall, the river tumbling from an imposing height half disclosed as it rips its tortuous way through canyon walls into your path. Now as waterfall after waterfall are periodically checked off your map, you come to a long-sought objective—the height of land.

After two weeks, ready to meet whatever the wilderness challenges, you make the long portage over one of the continent's great watersheds. It is long and rugged, made in short stages of a half mile at a time. A feeling of weariness—but also accomplishment—is the chief topic of conversation in camp that night. You have made the climb up the ocean's watershed.

Shelter is pitched on the bank of a creek that drains a large spruce bog. Through this narrow stream of water, you drift without effort—an impressive accumulation of water continuing to build up from every small trickle and incoming stream. The illusion of a tiny water-canoe route gradually begins to fade, as a dozen larger tributaries have combined to form a full-scale river, now flowing away from the ocean behind you, seeking its eager course down the inland watershed.

The rapidly increasing might of the river strikes you with sudden impact, when from a half mile ahead comes the thunderous roar of white water—the first descending rapids. Excitement runs high at the prospect of running through them. Here come the first severe tests of your skills as canoeists—the exacting proof of how well you can execute your canoe strokes, the sculling draw, quarter-sweep and others.

Wisdom calls for an appraisal of both the portage and the rapids. The trail is through tortuous granite crags, a punishing ordeal for two miles; so, you decide to risk running the cascade with the full load. It is a calculated risk, and you pause for a few anxious moments in the converging current above. Then, with wary resignation, you enter the point of no return—heart pounding at the thought of no longer having a choice. At each imposing bend in the river, as canyon walls loom up on either side, the course of the rapids begins to get more and more complicated, more violent; you must miss that giant swell to the right, swerve sharply to miss two others on the left, swing into the dark slicks whenever possible, and anticipate every hazard. Paddles whip from side to side, shiny wet blades flashing in the sun, because the sculling draw and the quarter-sweep must be executed on alternate sides to make the shifts from water race to water race.

The roaring rapids, arrogant and disdainful of human

The Rapids

life, are a din in your ears. But you want to shout as your
blood boils in the heat of battle. Scarcely a moment is allowed to glimpse the shore, yet a half-conscious sense of
sight through the outer perimeter of vision convinces you
that the forest is racing by. One moment you see your
partner in the bow, silhouetted against the sky; the next
moment he seems to be plunging into the trough of a
white-water wave. Then, in an instant, you find the canoe
floating serenely in the current below, the roar of the
rapids diminishing like the sound of a disappearing storm.

Now you take stock—the packs are almost floating in
water at the bottom of the canoe. Ashore, you unload,
you dry out. Smug expressions of victory are exchanged.
Across the canoe, shaking hands, you modestly assert,
"We made it."

5 FINDING THE WAY

THE fear of becoming lost has discouraged many aspiring canoeists, just as the lack of technical knowledge about navigating wilderness routes has been a major setback for many expeditions. Getting lost haunts the majority of hunters, who cling to tote roads and the parka tails of guides. Even most Indians and white woodsmen, who seem to have an uncanny ability to find the way in their own region, often fare badly in complex water areas, once they are beyond their own particular, familiar territory. The notion that some men have a special sense of direction and others do not, that Indians and other native, ethnic groups enjoy an infallible knack in finding their way, has been proved false.

One man can find his way better than another in remote areas simply because he has a greater capacity for observing and following clues. Men of all races who live permanently in the wilderness develop an ability to spot natural, directional clues. Considerable research has gone into the study of man's sense of direction, and the results have been quite conclusive: He has no *innate* sense of direction.

Men who claimed to have a sense of direction were flown blindfolded into the arctic prairie, mountain, desert, and forest areas, on days of no wind and heavy overcast.

Their "sense" proved to be only the average of guesses based on the law of probability.

I questioned the results of this research until I made some tests of my own over the years. And then I became satisfied that I had no sense of direction, in a psychic or special sense. When a leading university gave a fairly exhaustive scientific test of this so-called sense, and discovered that it could only be an idle boast (and *I* tested even such boasts), I based my subsequent travel in the wilderness on the premise that something more than a "brain directional mechanism" was needed to keep my trails properly oriented. There are apparently only two ways to know direction: (1) by observation of natural directional clues with the five senses; (2) with instruments.

Once the false notion of a special directional sense is discarded, the individual learns to develop a capacity for travel by careful observation of natural phenomena and reading of instruments—an accomplishment which is in no way a special sense, but certainly special knowledge.

The individual's first experience in a wilderness canoe region—an area with fairly large and intricate waterways —is often a bit frightening. To begin with, he has carefully examined his canoe route on the provisional map. There he sees lake, river, and portage, in the aggregate, as he might from an airplane, his eye sweeping over an area of about sixty nautical miles. Yes, there in plain view on the map is the 25-mile lake, where on one end he is to embark; there, too, in a neat pattern over a few inches, are the fifteen islands, large and small. The route, he observes, leads between the two larger islands on the north side of the lake, then swings off into an arm of the lake to the northeast. What could be simpler?—he need only cast his eyes down the lake, see the two islands, and head for them. And beyond, there is the bay. So appears the pattern on the provisional map.

Then comes the revelation. When he reaches the embarkation point, he glances down the lake. No islands of any kind are visible. All appears to be mainland. On the map it was inches from starting point to the two large islands; but multiplied 253,440 times, it becomes many miles. Nevertheless, somewhere down there along the north shore, in the confusing haze of distance, are the islands, visually indistinguishable from mainland, but in fact, we may be sure, in every insular sense—islands. This isn't quite what was expected.

Many canoe trips have ended right there. The party would suddenly decide "just to camp on the lake and take it easy." Of course, one could hire the local Indian guide, witness to the apprehensive departure; he knows the territory for 50 miles. But better, start out as planned, forget visual illusions, and resort to compass directions.

The basic mistake is to believe that something tangible, like an island, point, or abutment, must be identified as a directional bearing. Just as the "sense of direction" misconception should be done away with, it is also advisable to disregard most landmarks and rely on compass bearings, which may be thought of as tangibly as a conspicuous rocky abutment, an island or other visible landmarks. Compass directions, of course, are not always reliable, but compass bearings are most often distinguishable.

A compass may be influenced by highly magnetic areas, and therefore give an incorrect reading, but most complaints about erratic compass action are grossly exaggerated, or are attributable to the traveler's confusion. Too many people save face by blaming their bad judgment on the compass. Using a compass near an iron belt buckle, outboard motor, gun, or other magnetic attraction can cause serious dislocation over a long route.

We often read that the needle points to magnetic north. This is in error; the needle actually doesn't point to anything. It lines up with, or parallels, the magnetic field of the earth. On an irregular line over the earth, called the agonic line, the needle of the magnetic compass parallels true north and south, and this line is indicated on provisional maps with "O." As you get closer to the North and South Magnetic Poles, the compass needle continues to line up with the magnetic field, but an extremely varied field, having all sorts of so-called "pointings." It can point north, south, east, west, toward the sky, or toward the center of the earth, depending on your location relative to the magnetic poles and the complex variation of the earth's magnetic field.

The difference between the needle's lining up with the magnetic field and true north is called compass variation, or declination. If you don't allow for this difference between true north and where the needle comes to rest, you can get into orientation trouble. On provisional canoe maps, this variation is shown for all areas, so you won't have any trouble in learning how much to allow for declination.

The map will also tell you if the compass variation is east or west of true north. Let us say, for example, that the variation for a particular area reads 8 degrees east. This means that your compass needle will come to rest 8 degrees east of true north. Alternately, if the variation reads 8 degrees west, your compass needle will, of course, come to rest 8 degrees west of true north.

One should not try to travel over large stretches of water, or attempt to find a portage trail at a far-distant irregular shore without allowing for this variation. In British Columbia and in Labrador, the compass can be off true north by roughly 20 degrees. It varies, of course, in different parts of the continent, so always check your variation on the map when using the compass.

If there is no compass variation indicated on your map, observe where the needle comes to rest in relation to the direction of the North Star (Polaris). This will give you a fairly close check on your variation, since the North Star

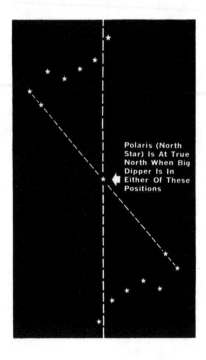

Polaris (North Star) Is At True North When Big Dipper Is In Either Of These Positions

is never more than about 1 degree off true north. To be more exact in your observation, check with the North Star when the star Alkaid, on the end of the handle of the Big Dipper, is either above or below the North Star, in the position shown in the illustration. Polaris is then at true north. You can do this best by driving two sticks into the ground, one short and one long, sharpening them to points with a knife, and aligning them with the North Star. Now, by placing your compass between the two sticks, see where the needle has come to rest. The difference in the stick alignment and the needle's pointing is your compass declination or variation for that area.

As an example of how far you can be off your proper direction without considering variation, each degree in compass variation error will throw you off your direction 1 foot for every 57.29 feet, more than 92 feet per mile. A compass variation of 8 degrees over a 10-mile distance of travel is likely to cause you to miss your objective, an error of more than ⅛ mile.

You can afford to be a bit lavish when you buy a compass. The best is not very expensive, and while the cheapest will hold a rough direction, what you want is one large enough to be clearly calibrated for all the 360 degrees of the circle. Cement your map to a piece of ⅛″ waterproof plywood, and coat it all with clear lacquer to make it waterproof. Place your compass on this cemented map when you work, so that you can calculate your position accurately.

Now make the correction between true north and where your needle comes to rest. Instead of referring to the four cardinal and intercardinal points of your compass as north, northeast, et cetera, use each of the 360 degrees on the dial as individual directions. For example, suppose that the direction of the route between two islands is northeast. On the ordinary sportsman's compass this direction would be calibrated as 45 degrees. If it was a bit off from northeast it could be any degree number around 42 or 48. (The term used is azimuth, which simply means direction.) Your direction would then be referred to as azimuth 42 or 48—or whatever degree direction you happened to use. Thus, any of the 360 degrees on the compass could at some time or place be a particular direction for you. If you think this is splitting hairs, consider that, to obtain accurate bearings, a surveyor divides the degree into 60 parts, called minutes; then, in turn, splits the minute up into 60 more parts, called seconds, with even a possible decimal point. But, if you stick approximately to whole degrees for canoe travel, you will come out all right.

In selecting a compass, you benefit if you ask for the cruiser type, which has the degrees calibrated on the dial counterclockwise, not clockwise as they appear on the sportsman's compass. After using a sportsman's compass, the cruiser's compass may seem confusing, but you will find the following cruiser plan is really simpler and allows greater general accuracy and convenience of travel.

On the inside of the cover on the cruiser's compass, you will see a straight, white-grooved line; this is called the "lubber's line." When the cover of the compass is open and turned back, this white line will provide a sight on your compass to distant objective points.

Let us say, after you orient your cruiser compass, and allow for declination, that your direction is 276, or azimuth 276. Simply rotate the compass box until the north end of the needle comes to rest over degree 276. Now your lubber's line is pointing in the proper direction, azimuth 276, a direction that happens to be slightly north of west. A few minutes of practice will overcome any initial difficulty, and you will be impressed by the practicability of this cruiser compass principle, once you have used it afield.

Do not attempt this cruiser compass procedure with the regular sportsman's compass. It will not work. On the regular sportsman's compass you can use the various degrees for directions, but you must first establish true north, using your correction for declination, and then read off the degree directions from the dial in the positions as they appear in their clockwise arrangement, not from where the needle comes to rest

Using simple compass directions, you should be able to get along fairly well with only map and compass in most mapped regions. If, however, you go a little beyond using a compass for simple directions alone, you will gain a marked advantage. In this further step, you will use your compass to create a line of position—a compass line drawn across your map in any direction, or a compass line sighted across the landscape. Your present position or any objective can be considered on a line of position. If you draw a second line of position, crossing the first, you will determine an exact point at the intersection of the two lines—a point which can be your position or any particular location. Finding a definite point by such transverse lines is called triangulation. This method can be used in various ways for establishing your position or for finding a particular position that is hard to locate on your canoe route. (See illustration showing two compass triangulation lines to mountain peaks for establishing a position.)

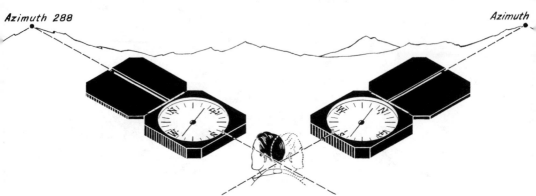

Sportsman's Compass—Triangulation to Two Mountain Peaks Using Lubber's Line on Compass Cover

For example, you are traveling over a wilderness lake, and 7 miles beyond a certain portage just made, you expect to come to a small river emptying into the lake on which you are traveling. Your route is planned to enter the mouth of this river and continue on its course. You assume that the river will certainly enter the lake along the north shore, so you feel you can neglect estimating the 7 miles and the river will be apparent when you reach it. However, the river may lie behind an island, in a marsh, behind a headland, or in some bay, where it will not be visible to you from the lake. Gradually, you discover that you have paddled longer than the time estimated to reach the river mouth, but no river is in sight. If the lake is irregular enough to have prominent points, or there are islands, which by their size or shape can be identified from your map, the river mouth can be located by noting on your map the relative compass line direction from the point or island to the river mouth, and then yourself sighting this compass line from the island. The river mouth will, of course, lie on this line of position.

Before you reached the mouth of the river, you would have taken a ruler (or other straight edge), and drawn a line on your map from a point which you could identify, to the mouth of the river, and would have noted the compass direction of this line on your map. If there are a number of similar islands and points, you may not be able to distinguish one from the rest. But this should not deter you from carrying out a line-of-position plan. To make sure that you do not miss the mouth of the river, you should draw not only one compass line on your map, but several lines from different positions to the mouth of the river, and note the directions, or azimuths, of the lines and where they intersect.

Now, as you approach the general area where you think the river should be, but you still do not see it, you can begin sighting with your compass from various islands, and check to see if these directions all converge on the mainland in the same manner as on your map. You can see that it would be almost impossible for a number of such lines of position to intersect at the shore of the lake just as they did on your map, and not designate the mouth of your river, regardless of whether or not you were able to identify the islands. The law of probability here would be too great for possible error.

This basic system of compass triangulation can be applied to numerous situations. If, for instance, your travel is on a mountain river, two distant mountain peaks, identifiable on the map, can be used to form lines of position by drawing lines from the peaks to any point on the map;

and the point where they intersect can be a position. If you sight two compass lines to peaks from your own position to find out how far you are from a certain point—and occasionally check the lines of position to these two mountain peaks for your own position as you travel—you will know by noting the intersection of the lines on your map where you are, how far you have gone, or how far you need to go. (See illustration of triangulation to two mountain peaks.)

These are, of course, simply elementary points to guide the average canoe traveler. The professional who has to fix exact positions will need instruments more accurate than the magnetic compass.

Fixing exact positions with technical instruments is clearly beyond the scope of this volume. The following general information is only for those who wish to enter into further study of the subject for use on scientific expeditions, where technical knowledge is required. Such knowledge, I might add, need not necessarily apply only to professional people. The canoe voyager who plans major trips into the wilderness should acquaint himself with more than the rudimentary information suggested above for the compass. A certificate in the sciences is not requisite for such learning.

Those who travel by canoe on rivers and lakes of the arctic far north, where magnetic compass readings are apt to be erratic, should have a solar compass, and make periodic observations to check the accuracy and declination of the magnetic compass. The solar compass will give azimuths by observation on any celestial body—sun, star, or planet. Ephemeris navigational data and accurate time by a transistor portable radio are needed for such computations.

If directions are to be required in the arctic far north during heavy overcast, a Polarized Phund Sky Compass should be part of the expedition's equipment.

Any canoe expedition whose members expect to do serious work in research, or other fields where exact positions or locations must be established, should use celestial navigation methods, employing a sextant and artificial horizon or a compact field transit. In rough, mountainous regions, where a great deal of elevation and triangulation work is to be done, along with celestial observations, the best instrument is the compact Explorer's Mountain Transit.

In most nonmountainous country, celestial observations for position can be made with a sextant, using the artificial horizon, since a natural horizon is not generally visible.

Travelers who are not familiar with advanced equipment are apt to shy away from such techniques. But celestial navigation has been greatly simplified in recent years, with altitude tables and other such shortcuts; and anyone who knows simple arithmetic can accomplish much. For example, what is difficult about the following? The altitude of the North Star above the horizon, in degrees and fractions of a degree—which can easily be measured by an amateur with a sextant and artificial horizon—is the approximate latitude. It requires only three small corrections from the *Nautical Almanac* to make the latitude more exact. Even this simple latitude line alone can serve as the base line or line of position for all operations.

Thus, the problem should not frighten a twelve-year-old boy. The reluctance to employ celestial navigation methods dates back to the time when altitude computations had to be worked out by spherical trigonometry. Obtaining longitude and making fixes for exact position, admittedly, are more involved than latitude observations, but not beyond the average layman with a knowledge of common arithmetic.

The voyager entering upon a long program of canoe travel will find calculating his position very interesting. And the confidence it inspires is inestimable—any area, no matter how unknown, offers no problem or risk of getting lost for the individual with this knowledge. He can move over every part of the earth's surface with confidence. The navigator is a welcome traveler with an expedition, and, after its leader, perhaps the most respected of the party.

Among Indians in long and remote travel, the navigator inspires confidence. A Cree chief in Canada once offered me his daughter in exchange for my sextant. Without explaining that it required special knowledge, I told him that I would be fortunate in the exchange, but both his beautiful daughter and I would get lost. He called me, in Cree: "The Man, Who on This Earth, Travels Among the Stars."

In Case of Accident

Without astronomical position finding, there is always some chance of becoming lost. Even with instruments, long cloudy periods can cause confusion. But more serious than being lost *with* full equipment and food is losing equipment or food—or both.

Canoes not properly pulled up may drift away. Sometimes a sudden storm will blow them into the water. Mice, intent upon getting salt deposited from sweaty hands on ropes, may gnaw through painters, and set a canoe adrift. Canoes, along with food and equipment, can be lost in rapids or heavy seas. If a canoe goes through a bad cascade after an upset, it can be damaged beyond repair.

You can reduce the risks to a minimum by careful, well-calculated operations. But when accidents do happen, it is well to know possible ways out.

The waterproof match safe should always be filled and kept in a pocket; the sheath knife should be on the belt; a coil of nylon leader and a couple of small spoon fishhooks, the points and barbs taped for protection, should be in the shirt pocket. With only these few items, you can travel far. The nylon leader will be useful both for rabbit snares and fishline. In a timbered area of lakes and rivers, you can now manage to obtain food and provide warmth at night for sleep. This will call for resourcefulness, but no specialized knowledge of woodcraft.

Snowshoe hares are generally abundant in the northern wilderness, especially at the height of the propagation cycle. In almost any thicket you will find their dung and runways. Any book on trapping will show a number of ways to set snares. The preferred method is to tie the snare to a bent-over sapling, the sapling hooked in a notch you have cut in another sapling. The first tug by the snared hare releases the sprung sapling and hangs him.

Fishing should be done, if possible, at the foot of falls or cataracts and in deep, narrow water. The nylon line with a spoon dangling at the end should be attached to a slim pole cut from the forest. Do not weight the spoon hook, but let it sink slowly, and then troll it with short jerks through the eddies. In virgin waters, results are almost certain.

When preparing the fish, cut through the back, not the belly, to the intestinal tract, and open the fish like a book. Peel and sharpen some sticks for skewers. Force them through the fish for support, then prop the fish up before an open fire and bake about six inches away from active flames.

If no fish are available, use your shirt to catch minnows or crawfish. Button the shirt, and tie the neck shut. This will form a baglike net. Tie the open bottom end of the shirt to a long crotched stick in the manner of a scoop net, and work through the eddies and along the shore. Spread the minnows or crawfish on a sheet of birch bark, and roast them just enough to make them palatable, or boil them. For boiling, make a receptacle out of birch bark by heating it and turning up the sides, holding the folds intact with "clothespins" made from split sticks. Water will come to a boil in such a utensil supported over a fire without burning the birch bark, but you can speed up the operation by dropping in hot stones periodically. Use a forked stick for handling the stones. Minnows and fish can, of course, be eaten raw. For preserving, fish can be dried. Split open as in baking; hang with spruce roots or deciduous bark strip slings on a frame in the sun, or—better—in the sun high above a slow smoking fire, burning poplar or barkless birch. Green birch will burn once the fire is well under way.

Rock tripe, a flat lichen that grows on rocks of the north, can be eaten. It contains about 40 percent starchy food, and must be roasted thoroughly before an open fire to prevent gastric disturbance. The inner bark of the poplar tree when cooked gives off a somewhat nourishing gelatinous food. Remove the fiber after cooking, and eat the jelly. Experiment with various underwater and upland plant roots, but always try a small amount first and wait fifteen minutes, or longer, for possible unpleasant reaction before consuming any substantial amount.

Look for frogs along rush-grown sandy beaches or marshy areas. Almost any creature is edible. If you come upon a lumbering porcupine, easily killed with a stick, you will have food for several days. Rodents and snakes are edible. When you have missed enough meals, you won't be fussy.

The Lumbering Porcupine

If there are extended periods of hunger, drink water as often as you can to carry off the poisons that accumulate in the body when there is no normal elimination.

The chief problem of travel in canoe country without a water craft is to get across lakes and rivers. Seek the narrows whenever possible. When a wide water crossing has to be made, drag any deadwood you can find to the waterfront for a raft. Dig out spruce roots for lashing the pieces together, and supplement these roots, if necessary, with ties made from your own clothing. Find a long pole for propelling your craft; it need not always touch bottom, and will work as a paddle. Your body may be partly submerged on this craft, but you will get across the water.

Get as much sleep as possible, and try to dispel any feelings of panic. If you have sufficient food—of any sort— and can get through the nights with reasonable rest, your chance of survival is very high. Even if you have no food, but you do have water and rest, you can live a long time on the natural nourishment stored in your body tissues.

If there are long periods between eating, take in only small amounts when food is accessible. And when you reach the outside, having starved for a considerable period, eat small amounts, and rest between meals. If you gorge yourself, the consequent cramps will be worse than the hunger.

6 PORTAGE TRAILS

PORTAGE trails are not often direct routes between two bodies of water. Usually they are twisting, undulating paths of natural design, stippled by countless moccasined feet through the centuries upon the forest floor.

A straight line—supposedly the shortest distance between two points—would thus by any law of natural selection rarely be the best route for a portage trail. Portage trails wander, but not aimlessly, for in one place a boulder or root must be avoided, in another an insurmountable contour.

Approaches to portage trails sometimes provide good camping areas. Other approaches are on floating bogs, or cramped against a steep declivity of solid rock where you must claw your way with heavy loads up steep, narrow inclines. Where rapids are numerous along a river, such as the Berens River in Manitoba, Canada, some of the portages may bear in so close to the upper end of rapids as to make embarkation a frantic paddle to escape from being carried into the white water.

The bank of a tiny stream trickling through the forest may provide a good inland camp, especially desirable on cold, windy days, but not, of course, in the fly season. After thirty miles of paddling a canoe through river and

The Portage Trail

lakes without an interrupting land mass, it is not strange to come upon so appropriate a name as "Diversion Portage," and so rugged is Diversion Portage that the lake it reaches is called "Diversion Lake." Lakes and portage trails both may thus alternately provide happy relief to a weary canoe voyager.

How do portage trails begin? How old are they? Combining conjecture with reasonable deductions, we can presume that the first trails were made by animals. Animals, both small and large, travel between bodies of water, even in winter when trails lead over land and ice. The first human beings to use portage trails probably traveled along wildlife trails, stumbled upon successive lakes, then altered the trails for convenience.

Carbon 14 tests and other modern processes may one day soon disclose some of the secrets hidden in the ancient campfire remains of these camps. We may be able to learn when and how certain portage trails and camps originated, and perhaps something about the earliest animal inhabitants and the people who first broke trail over these areas.

Rapid growth of vegetation in lands of heavy rainfall can soon obliterate wilderness trails, and it is safe to assume that once trails have been made, animals play the most important role in keeping them from becoming overgrown. Aerial contour surveys and actual use have only on rare occasions shown established wilderness portage trails to be unnecessarily long or misplaced. Normally, surprising ingenuity is seen in the original selection of routes for portage trails, especially in the unique and involved bypasses which must have required thorough knowledge of the areas.

Almost fifty years ago, when aerial mapping was unheard of, and other surveys were limited, I came upon an unusual portage at a waterfall that dropped through a canyon. While portage trails up to this point had been well used by the Indians, none was apparent below the falls. There was no possible way to scale the slippery, rocky slopes around the falls with a heavy pack load or a canoe on my shoulders. It took me several hours of wide ranging over the area to discover the solution. A quarter of a mile back from the water route I had come was a trail that led inland away from the river to a small stream. The stream then led to the river above the cascade half a mile from the point of its descent into the canyon, an easy though circuitous route. Primitive man must have been very familiar with the region to figure out this ingenious bypass.

Nature does not always provide terrain for convenient portage trails. In some places where such trails must start or end, almost sheer, rocky abutments form the shores. In one spot in Minnesota, the Forestry Service has provided wooden stairs for a steep portage trail; and if I remember correctly, it required 120 steps. On canoe maps it is referred to as "Stairway Portage." Deeper in the wilderness, no such luxuries as wooden stairways exist. On wet days, when mossy slopes make the footing treacherous, it may even be necessary to use tracking lines from the top of such approaches to hoist the canoe and packs over the rock abutment, or crawl on hands and knees over eskers.

My nervous system is not attuned to steeplejack maneuvers. It is not a comforting prospect to think of carrying a canoe along a narrow, canyon-wall trail, or across an improvised log bridge, with a roaring cataract below, while the wind buffets the bow and stern from side to

Now Each Step Over a Portage Trail Has Become a Bit More Precise

side. Indeed, it is an experience most of us will momentarily try to forget when we realize that we must go back over these tongue-parching hazards to pick up the rest of the load at the beginning of the trail. Such are a few portages on the trails of some mountain rivers in British Columbia, in the Yukon Territory, and in Alaska. In the same regions, strangely enough, are pleasant trails through forests as serene, safe, and unobstructed as the water routes of forest plains.

One recalls with pleasant reflection the watercourses of lakes and rivers, where island after island, point after point, slipped by in a procession of overwhelming beauty. But entering the green mansions of portage trails with a pack or a canoe, not knowing what lies beyond, guided entirely by the route itself is likely to become the most impressive memory; exactly why, I am unable to say.

A shouldered canoe will shut out much of the view along a portage trail. Each portaging step requires undivided attention if perfect balance and ease of movement are to be maintained. The trail may ascend a gentle rocky rise over a hogback of granite, drop somewhat abruptly into a glen, wander over exposed roots and down timber, skirt marshy places and puddles of water. Then it may begin to climb a gradual slope, dodge boulders the size of a room, elbow its way through shoulder-high rock cleavages and a dense growth of jackpine. The canoe barely clears the cramped curves. Breath finally gets short, and you wonder how much of this rough terrain is still ahead.

Then perhaps you stagger onto a rise, where a plateau of solid granite prevents the growth of any plant life. At one side of the trail is a perpendicular rock, cracked by centuries of frost. Here in a cleft you lean the canoe for a rest, and take stock of the area. Shoulders rejoice in the freedom from their heavy load. Even though the temperature is 50, there is delight in the luxury of a gentle breeze in this small forest opening.

The canoe, rubbing against resinous coniferous boughs, has screeched and lamented every minute—like a coot out of water. Until now, it has muffled all natural sounds of the trail. For a moment the yellow leaves of a small-toothed aspen flutter in the transient breeze. Then silence. Ten days ago the Canadian National Railway trains could be heard roaring through the rock cuts of the Pre-Cambrian Shield. Now their sounds are completely lost by distance.

You become immobile and silent in the awesome quiet of this small forest arena. The least noise or movement seems sacrilegious. The aspen leaves quiver audibly again for a moment, then settle into utter stillness as though making inquiry and then listening for an answer. Is it possible that there are cities and towns—people engaged in daily activity, something called civilization somewhere upon the earth? The only answer—the occasional soft flutter of the leaves. But although the silence seems to hold all in suspense, protesting action, you remember that a canoe is to be portaged.

For another quarter mile the trail is relatively easy, over barren rock and into jackpine forest. Suddenly, the trail descends, becomes rougher, favors a terrain that seems to be a poor choice of contour. Any other direction you feel to be a more logical course. Off to one side is smoother ground, but the trail dictates that the easier terrain is not the way of the wilderness. Every step now must be carefully considered. Down, only down it leads, and through the worst kind of footing.

Suddenly, you hear a roar that is almost deafening. You

feel a spray, and water begins to drip from your nose. The trail becomes more and more slippery. And, it is getting rougher. A few moments ago you could not imagine this to be possible. Then you see it—a violent cascade, thundering down over the roughest bedrock in the world. At the foot of the falls the portage trail ends abruptly on a large sheet of granite, glazed by countless ages of flood, low water, and spray.

A hundred yards of eddy, foam, and boiling maelstrom project from the foot of the cataract, but soon the water levels off to the quiet surface of a bay, lying deep, dark, and ominous below the surrounding rocky hills.

On the return over the portage trail you wonder how the noise of this booming cataract can diminish so quickly in the dense forest. The wind and the canyon walls have something to do with it, of course, but the acoustical effect of the forest is the greatest muffler of all.

Without the canoe, the trail back does not seem so rough. You grow anxious to tell your partner about the magnificence and wonder of what you have discovered.

In the Far North on portage trails there are few chance meetings of human beings. A man could starve to death waiting for help. I once stopped at a trapper's cabin off to one side of a portage trail in Manitoba's wilderness, and found a note tacked to his door, "Back in two days." I waited. He returned that evening, having been gone two days. I stayed three days.

Four years later I made the same canoe journey and stopped again. On the door was another note which read: "Cutting wood down river. Back tonite." When I hunted him up, he lost all interest in woodcutting, and wanted to talk. "How many people have come this way in the four years since I stopped?" I inquired. "A few Indians and a Mountie," he slowly recalled. In four years the notes on his door had been addressed to these few people.

Several years later the trapper was flown out for burial. Somewhere on the outside, he had a sister. One of his sled dogs, trailing part of a chewed-off harness, had shown up, half starved, at an Indian camp 60 miles away. The man's body was found bloated and half frozen in the thawing and freezing ice of a creek, where he had broken through and drowned.

In 1919 I met another trapper on a portage trail in Ontario. He was carrying a cast-iron kitchen range on his back with a tumpline, a 5-gallon can of kerosene in one hand, a gallon pail of pancake syrup in the other. On my own back was a packsack load of provisions and camp equipment topped with a bedroll, a small load by comparison. We were both anxious for a little talk. Neither put down his load. Our heads pitched forward, tugging at our tumplines, we must have resembled a couple of fighting cocks about to attack.

He had a winter's supply of provisions in his canoe. That evening we were camped at opposite ends of the portage, scheduled to leave the next morning on our separate routes. But we visited, drank tea, and fed the fire far into the night. We did not depart as planned. A friendship had developed. I carried all my equipment again to his end of the portage. Then we traveled for nine days over lake, river, and portage routes, to reach his cabin. Shortly after Christmas, before the snow began to lie too deep, I left with some Indians by dog team for the outside. In April of the following spring I returned by dog team and came out by canoe.

Spring Breakup—Out by Canoe

Wilderness forest, with obstructing down-timber, rocky terrain, and underbrush, does not generally allow free travel afoot. Game trails in remote wilderness areas permit some foot travel, but they rarely lead in the desired direction. Thus, the urge to reach a closer intimacy with the deep forest is most often satisfied on portage trails. Here, I think, lies their special lure—portage trails are the few avenues of penetration into the inner sanctum of Nature.

In my youth, when I felt more accomplishment in the flexing of muscles than in careful observation, I hurried over portage trails. Now I am more inclined to linger and observe, though pressure of getting heavy packs and canoes overland sometimes compels haste. Relaxation and a chance for observation come as one returns for the second load. Canoe voyages of any significant length may call for more than one trip over a portage—the average long journey, two or more trips.

Most portage trails are moist, and therefore silent underfoot. The eye and ear must be constantly alert if you are to observe wildlife. Partridge, especially in the fall of the year, seem to enjoy the more open areas of portage trails. Those you see are often standing motionless in your very path. It is possible that they have never seen a human being. In fact, brood following brood may have been hatched and reared in the interval of two journeys over the portage. To one side of the trail in the forest, though only 10 feet away and in open view, partridge may not even be visible. Their mottled, somber coloring blends perfectly with the forest, and they know instinctively that immobility to the very last moment of risk before flight is their best protection.

Partridge Standing Motionless

Surprise a Couple of Black Ducks Feeding in the Bay

If the ground happens to be soft and silent, and the wind is right, it is not uncommon for you to meet a bear, moose, woodland caribou, or other animal on the portage trail. You come to a halt; so does he. You stare at each other for a few moments. If the animal has not already caught your scent, the chances are he will turn off the trail, and slowly lumber away into the deep forest. But in his apparent uncertainty as to what kind of creature you are, he may circle to get your scent and then you will hear him crashing off without hesitation. Much of the wildlife on the portage trail you will not see at all. The animals see you, or hear you, or catch your scent long before you detect their presence.

When portages are long and unfamiliar, the far end of the trail often promises a refreshing relief in the opening panorama of a new lake. On the last turn when you see the first flash of blue wilderness water, every faculty comes alive. Frequently, your approach surprises a couple of black ducks feeding in the immediate bay. As they take off, quacking their danger signal, loons farther out on the water pick up the warning and begin sounding off the most engaging call in all the North. And still farther down the lake you hear other loons calling in relay, until the forest walls resound for miles, with the echoes.

Far off in the hazy distance, through island after island, headland after headland, possibly in some remote bay, lies your trail through a land of silent places. But now you are content to stow the packs in the canoe, and enter upon the magnificence of another wilderness lake—a quiet interlude before the threatening roar of some river that leads to a new adventure, a new mood, another portage.

7 SOME SIGNIFICANT CANOE VOYAGES

A COMMENDABLE endeavor of canoeists in recent years has been to retrace the canoe routes of early explorers. Those having a keen eye for observing significant geographical and natural factors along canoe routes could help clear up a few of the existing enigmas in historical material. A significant development in this direction has come about in the discovery of large quantities of fur trade goods and native artifacts by skin diving methods in the rapids of wilderness rivers. Setting up camp on the spot where a famous explorer slept, you experience a strange, romantic sensation, as though you were being projected into the past.

A single chapter, surely, can touch on very few canoe voyages; but the following descriptions should provide background material, and point up some of the problems to be considered in wilderness canoe travel.

Many years ago I was intrigued by the idea of examining an area of water, located roughly at the juncture of 90 degrees, 30 minutes west longitude, and the Canadian-United States boundary—the route traveled by Alexander Mackenzie. He describes the lake bottom here as muddy and slimy, but with three or four feet of clear water over it. He tells of probing the depths with a 12-foot pole, meeting no more resistance than if the mud and slime were just water. And he goes on to claim that this water produced so strong a suction that he had great difficulty paddling away from the powerful attraction even with the aid of six energetic paddlers, and that he had heard there was grave danger of canoes being swallowed up.

Mackenzie, a man, no doubt, of extraordinary imagination, was apparently subject to a share of superstition, for I paddled over the area a number of times, and while I found the suspended mud and slime, and marveled at the sharp demarcation between the clear and silted water, I felt no hint of suction or attraction—paddling was as easy here as anywhere. Yet to this day there are travelers who approach this area with apprehension, and even insist that they managed to cross over it only with great difficulty.

No such tales can possibly detract from the magnificence and courage of Mackenzie's highly important voyages, which breached the Great Unknown through the Mackenzie River to the Arctic Ocean, and west to the Pacific. He continually faced the hazards of uncertainty and hostile Indians. Traveling every water mile by canoe and paddle—sustaining himself largely by whatever provisions he was able to find en route by hunting and fishing —Alexander Mackenzie's undertaking is certainly worthy of our greatest admiration.

The canoe journeys of Lewis and Clark through the Missouri and other waters through the mountains to the West Coast, those of Samuel Hearne into the Coppermine River to the Arctic, and many more give the history of North America a special kind of narrative—a rich background of exploration intrigue that provides a valuable historical and literary complement for present-day canoe voyagers.

Little is gained by just putting miles and periodic camps behind. We need to move slowly and carefully, watching for any detail of information and interest. A daily diary can become the treasure of later life.

Early journeys tend to be forgotten until modern historians dig them out of the archives and revitalize them. On the other hand, more recent or contemporary journeys and the people who make them are bound, somehow, to seem more real. Four of these journeys have a pattern, I think, of special significance here.

The Hubbard–Wallace–Elson Voyage

Around the beginning of the century—just a few years before I made my first major canoe trip—Elbert Hubbard and Dillon Wallace embarked on their fateful canoe journey into Labrador. George Elson, a half-breed Cree Indian from James Bay, was the third member of the party. He was, Wallace said, not only a very competent woodsman, but a hero as well.

The purpose of Hubbard's canoe journey was to explore the little-known region of Labrador from Hamilton Inlet to Lake Michikamau—the primary objective being to reach Lake Michikamau, which stretched inviolate for 90 miles over an uncharted wilderness.

The Naskaupi River, their scheduled route to Michikamau, emptied into Grand Lake. But they somehow missed seeing its mouth and, with fatal consequences, entered another wide-mouthed river—to quote Wallace, "the dreadful Susan Valley." Its numerous rapids gave it the appearance of the river described to them as the Naskaupi. The Susan was eventually destined to lead them into much suffering through fatigue and starvation. Because of the very short Labrador summer at this high latitude, encroaching winter caught them unprepared. The return journey ended in tragedy: Hubbard succumbed to the ordeal of exposure and starvation, and died before they reached the outside.

Michikamau's shores were not attained, but over a high promontory which Hubbard and Elson had climbed, they had a long view into the distance and there saw Michikamau in all its glory—a great and magnificent expanse of water, and yet, a mocking sea of defiance and frustration.

Had they found the mouth of the Naskaupi River, a wholly different story might have been told—but certainly not one of greater human significance than the tragedy of the Susan.

The Hubbard–Wallace voyage had its critics, but largely those with invidious hindsight. Hubbard, Wallace and Elson were responsible woodsmen, and their taking the wrong river cannot be adjudged in terms of what is now known about the geography of the region. Any of us who has navigated the complex waters of the Canadian wilderness can readily see how such a mistake can be made. They had been told that the Naskaupi River came into a bay at the *end* of Grand Lake. As they moved along they saw the bay into which the Naskaupi flowed, but it seemed a less natural choice with Grand Lake continuing on with more imposing water. Wallace said that Hubbard rose up in the canoe for a view of the bay they were passing and remarked, "Oh, that's just a bay and it isn't worth while to take time to explore it. The river comes in here at the end of the lake. They all said it was at the *end* of the lake."

But, ironically, Grand Lake has a three-toed claw shape

at the west end which receives four rivers, in bays of almost equal prominence. Wallace carried a sextant, and here of all places it should have been used. But perhaps the sky was overcast, and the confidence any voyage holds at the start apparently fired them to go on. Most often an important river coming into the end of a bay alone drains the region. Here was one of the exceptions. There seem to be times when the odds in a given circumstance weigh heavily toward making the cardinal error. This, obviously, was one of those times.

Wallace later returned and made a successful voyage. At the same time, another canoe party made the journey, presumably set on outdoing him. Wallace, a sensitive and intelligent man, showed no interest in traveling the wilderness as a race. The competition reached their destination ahead of Wallace, but, to their surprise, he continued on, even after the snows came, over a successful dog sled trip to the "outside," while his apparently disconcerted adversaries took to the comfort of a ship.

The Hubbard-Wallace-Elson expedition is remembered not for the controversy or derision of others that ensued but for the deep relationship among three men who endured unto death an adventure of the Labrador Trail.

The Taylor–Pope Expedition

A canoe voyage of great length with special significance for the apprehensive wilderness traveler was made in 1936–1937 by Sheldon P. Taylor and Geoffrey W. Pope, from New York to Nome, Alaska—a distance of 7,000 miles. Especially notable is that, except for the 150 miles of portages, the entire trip was made by paddle—not by outboard motor.

Early fur trade inspectors and others traveled season after season, from breakup to freeze-up, over canoe routes of the continent, until their accumulated mileage through the years became fabulous. But the first year's travel by Taylor and Pope—from New York to Fort Smith in a single season, and from Fort Smith to Nome the second season—is a most impressive record. Taylor was twenty-five and Pope twenty-three when they made the trip—without guides.

Pope has told me that, surprisingly, the most difficult part of the voyage was from New York to Montreal—a fact that should allay some of the fears of canoeists who wonder whether they can travel safely in remote wilderness regions.

Here were two young men, working in offices in New York, who became restless, and decided, initially, to take a canoe trip to Montreal. Young men in many parts of the country make such plans every season, but this was not destined to be a plan so limited. At the port of New York, they had access to the Export Department's atlas. Maps, everyone knows, have a way of reducing a whole continent to a mere eyeful.

"Why not go all the way to Alaska?" one of them mused.

One might suspect that such high-reaching aspirations had momentarily overcome their better judgment. But not with the zeal of these young men. They owned a dilapidated canoe which surely could not—and, in fact, did not—make the whole journey. But they started out in it from New York's Forty-second Street Dock, paddled up the Hudson River to Lake Champlain, through the Richelieu River to the St. Lawrence River, and finally arrived in Montreal.

By the time they reached Montreal, their journey had captured the imagination of the country through the newspaper publicity of Walter Winchell and other newsmen. Curious throngs gathered at the waterfront to welcome them.

But the trip might well have ended at Montreal had these been ordinary young men, for by the time they reached Montreal, they had learned an important thing about wilderness travel—the complexity of protracted companionship. This, their first experience with "bushiness" (backwoods psychosis), almost convinced them to terminate the trip at Montreal. This decision became impossible under the circumstances. In addition to the personal remorse they would have suffered, they couldn't lose face before a world waiting to see them meet the challenge of going all the way to Alaska by canoe.

Taylor and Pope reasoned that through several centuries of the fur trade, men had traveled in the wilderness together through long periods of confinement in a canoe and small tent. So, not to be outdone, they came up with a possible solution.

They drew their own special "ten commandments"— rules of conduct which they thought would apply to every possible occasion. But, as Pope has pointed out since, their ten commandments were not, and could never be, functional.

"Nothing works," he said, "when men get 'bushed.' It's the next thing to insanity. It can happen to anyone—the most logical and rational minds, the kindest and most tolerant people of any age."

However, Pope noted, the ten commandments did have

the distinct value of making them continually aware that they could get "bushed." And by accepting the fact that two men living so closely over an extended period without the relief of other association, or even privacy, will inevitably create conflict, they were able to be more or less objective and rational about their problem. Thus, they managed with some success to curb their feelings.

Those who had refused to sponsor the Taylor–Pope journey at the start, because they did not wish to be "linked with possible failure," now revised their deprecating attitude, and forwarded a $400 check to the voyagers at Montreal. A new canoe was purchased. Taylor and Pope left Montreal, as crowds of well-wishers cast flowers upon the water—the traditional honor due explorers. They continued over the historic fur trade route, up the Ottawa River to the Mattawa River, and through the Mattawa to Lake Nipissing to Georgian Bay—the northern arm of Lake Huron. Following the coast of Georgian Bay to Sault Ste. Marie, and along the shore of Lake Superior, they reached the mouth of the Pigeon River, between Minnesota and Ontario.

Traditionally, the fur trade route continued along the shore of Lake Superior to Grand Portage, a famous center of the early trade, situated on the shore of Lake Superior a dozen or so miles from the mouth of the Pigeon River, where a 9-mile portage was made by the fur traders to avoid the numerous shallow rapids of the Pigeon. But Taylor and Pope thought it less arduous to wade or track their shallow-draft canoe and outfit through the shoals of the river than pack it 9 miles overland, over a trail that was then pretty well grown over.

The headwaters of the Pigeon River are at South Fowl Lake, where the chain of lakes continues across the boundary between Minnesota and Ontario, to form what is deservedly called "canoe country." Leaving the lake chain, they traveled into Rainy River and through the river into Lake of the Woods, the French Lac du Bois.

So far, their route had been in and out of the United States and Canada, but at Lake of the Woods it entered Canada abruptly, and went along the Winnipeg River, which flows into Lake Winnipeg. The lake narrows down about a hundred miles north at what is known as Long Point, allowing a reasonably safe canoe crossing to the west shore for a northern access to the mouth of the Saskatchewan River. Through the Saskatchewan River they continued over the famous Frog and the Methy portages of fur trade history—the latter a 13-mile-long carry over the watershed. The Mackenzie River system was then reached, where their route was once more downstream.

At Fort Smith, winter overtook the voyagers. Open-water canoe travel ended, as every northern body of water (except the ocean) was imprisoned in ice. Taylor and Pope saw no practical way to remain confined in a cabin through a long northern winter, and survive the imminent conflict of exclusive association.

Both men, however, displayed resourcefulness and perseverance. They sought out two trappers operating in different territories, who were willing to accept them individually as helpers and companions. Thus, separated, they passed the winter amicably, and also expanded their experience and knowledge of woodcraft. This simple arrangement is an interesting aspect of the treatment of "bush psychosis," although marked differences in temperament were no doubt factors.

In the spring, the voyage was resumed. Pope told me that a wonderful feeling of congeniality existed between

Taylor and himself for about two weeks. Then, gradually, the grueling tension and friction of wilderness travel built up again.

This tension increased when they reached Great Slave Lake, and found that the ice had not yet gone. In order to keep traveling and avoid the pall and friction of a permanent camp, they dragged their canoe over ice mass after ice mass, and into spring-thawed lead after lead. Moving the canoe over the rough ice was comparable to walking over ice-coated, rough gravel and boulders, said Pope. To avoid damaging the canoe in the outgoing ice, they pushed their craft onto floating ice masses riding them as rafts, and thus managed to drift with the spring breakup through the first part of the great Mackenzie River.

In the complex arctic delta, the problem confronting them was to find where the Rat River entered the Mackenzie—difficult enough in normal water, but made even more complex in floodtime. Travel had now brought them to a point 300 miles north of the Arctic Circle. The Rat River, dropping 1,200 feet in 40 miles, allows only an arduous passage via McDougall's Pass across the mountains. At the source of the Rat River is tundra, where three small lakes, referred to as The Summit Lakes, continue passage into the Little Porcupine River, not more than a creek, but a body of water that eventually paid off for Pope and Taylor, for it empties into the last of the rivers on their route—the mighty, long-sought Yukon.

For approximately a thousand miles the Yukon promised travel downstream, but the broad reaches of this river soon dispelled any thoughts of an easy drift. It necessitated long days of weary work with paddles, especially as they encountered head-on winds. Nevertheless, they enjoyed the consolation of being on a river that held in its long water the final hope of success. At the mouth of the Yukon River they paddled through a school of beluga whales, a fitting and spectacular reception to the Bering Sea. Since their destination was Nome, they still had to travel 300 miles of Alaska's coast in water certainly not styled for a small canoe. Nevertheless, they were determined, and there came a moment, at last, when the concluding paddle stroke was made—and they stepped out upon the beach at Nome.

The Taylor-Pope canoe journey, I think, holds a great deal for the modern-day canoe traveler's consideration especially concerning the psychological and physical problems of two men in close association on a long journey. Most commendable in the Taylor-Pope conduct was their meeting the challenges and proving equal to them.

The Sevareid-Port Youthful Adventure

The canoe journey from Minneapolis to York Factory on Hudson Bay by Arnold E. Sevareid (better known to most of us as Eric Sevareid, the ace journalist) and Walter C. Port, at the close of their high school years, is a heart-warming story of youthful trial and error that is bound to thrill anyone with a feeling for adventure. When Stefansson the explorer said that "adventure is the result of incompetence," perhaps he meant more pointedly that inexperience creates misadventure.

Whatever may be said about the Sevareid and Port travels, the boys did not lack aspiration or determination. A strange world can be a frightening world, and the North was a strange world to these youths. Coping daily with problems that are totally unfamilar certainly makes for a wide range of human error. This error was realistic enough in the Sevareid-Port trip, but with it went a great share of courageous trial: and the fact that they reached their destination—somehow—indicated a large measure of trial and *success*.

After the boys had harried the *Minneapolis Star* newspaper for a week to sponsor the trip, its managing editor decided to back their venture. They were to send in a running story at every possible mailing point.

"Never, never had we been so excited!" said Sevareid. "People stopped to stare at the two of us, one long and lean, the other short and stocky, galloping through the streets, talking as fast as we could with both our mouths and all our hands."

On June 17, 1930, they pushed the *Sans Souci*, an Old Towne, 18-foot, canvas canoe, into the Mississippi River, rode a mile in the fast current, then turned into the channel of the Minnesota River. They had gained information from camping manuals, written by not very realistic authors, who gave such dogmatic advice as always to camp near a spring. But sewers and drainage ditches flowed like springs along one of the nation's historic rivers, tragically polluted by the towns along its banks.* The first big segment of their journey was not altogether a happy one, if any teen-age adventure can ever be disenchanting.

The Minnesota River, with its muddy banks, dips far to the south before it turns north to join the Mississippi, meandering through a farming region, with hairpin curves, adding further distance to the already misguided course of the river. Here, on the Minnesota River their

* A vigorous pollution-elimination program is now under way by the Minnesota River Recreation Development Association.

trip became a succession of rescues—sheep and cattle were mired to their middles along the muddy banks; but the boys also met generous, warmhearted people. Best of all, they were daily being hardened to the trail. Port, with a little more natural upholstery than Sevareid, did not find the ground a hard bed; but Sevareid, raw-boned, admits freely that he did not sleep well those first nights.

They had been paddling against the current in the Minnesota River, and at Lake Traverse they entered the Red River. While it flows north, it offered no relief by a drift in the twisting and sluggish current.

On crossing the boundary into Canada, they saw a lone deer—Sevareid's first—a special welcome into the north-land. At the Canoe Club in Winnipeg, they were introduced to both discouragement and encouragement. Local people have a tendency to exaggerate the dangers of their region, so Sevareid and Port found little trouble in some of the waters the natives had pronounced dangerous. Eventually, they began to use their own judgment in weighing the purported dangers and suggested advantages.

Having traveled Lake Winnipeg in a canoe, I can appreciate the feeling that Sevareid and Port had when they left the river, and came out upon the immense waters of this lake. It is a shallow lake for a body of water so extensive, which means that it can become very rough. As Sevareid said, "It might as well have been the Atlantic Ocean." A canoe shrinks to insignificance in the immensity of these heavy seas, the breakers rolling in from the horizon. This is a lake of reefs that often lie treacherously just below the surface, hazards made worse by the dark, unclear, clay-silted water. One plans to follow the shore a safe distance out, but this becomes quite impossible, since reefs extend far out into the lake and must be bypassed seaward. Then, there are numerous deep bays, which pose a gamble: to travel, you must choose between a course far out into the perilous open water for a shortcut from point to point, or double the traveling distance by following closely the meandering shore.

These lads caught on quickly to the various tricks of survival in heavy seas: side-wall tilting the canoe just far enough to allow a breaker to hit a broad freeboard; paddlers relaxed at the hips, riding and rolling with the canoe. Neither had much previous experience. Learning by trial and error in dangerous water is not a simple process, for mistakes rarely allow a second chance.

When they neared Balsam Bay, Sevareid, who had been born and raised on the prairies, was thrilled by the beauty of the evergreen forest stretching for miles along a rockbound shoreline with periodic sand beaches. Islands of granite, with a few decorative spruce and birch trees softening their ruggedness, dotted the lake on to infinity.

At Victoria Beach they brought the canoe into a little wind-sheltered cove and camped for the night. Here they came closer to the true elements of the North, the lake heaving defiantly out beyond the cove, the forest rising wild and mysterious only a few yards away.

Harrowing experiences with Lake Winnipeg were to continue as they followed along the east shore, encountering the continual hazards of close calls while encircling the reefs and spanning the deep bays. Frequently they became windbound, and could not travel at all. Seeing Indians confidently traveling along the lake in small canoes gave Sevareid and Port the courage to take off in their own small craft, even when their judgment suggested laying up for calmer weather.

Indian camps appeared along the shore, where sled dogs

were tethered to trees, far enough apart to be safe from each other's menacing jaws. The dogs bared their teeth, howled, and tugged at their leashes as Sevareid and Post paddled by.

At Berens River settlement they came in contact with the romance typical of wilderness outposts. Located on the steam-vessel route from Winnipeg, Berens River Post supplies by canoe other posts in the interior—Pekangikum and Little Grand Rapids. Stationed at Berens River are Mounted Police—more accurately in this section today, police who travel in rugged freight canoes, bush planes, by dog sled, motorized toboggan, and snowmobile, although little mechanization existed at the time Sevareid and Port made their journey.

The boys might have taken this Berens River route over the watershed to other rivers flowing into Hudson Bay, rather than the Nelson and Gods rivers. And I'm not sure why they didn't, for the prevailing fall winds began to blow from the North, churning Lake Winnipeg into great breakers. Sevareid, looking out upon the threatening waters, suggested that the trip from Berens River to Warren's Landing, at the northeast end of the lake, be made on the *Wolverine*, a passenger freighter. They tossed a coin (their solution to part of the friction problem) and the *Wolverine* won.

Less hardy individuals might have ended the journey at Berens River; five hundred miles of river and small lake travel by canoe remained after leaving the *Wolverine*, before they would reach their destination at York Factory. The trip was a long way from its end. Naturally, they were disappointed in not being able to continue all the way by canoe. The boys were aware that any party traveling by canoe in the North, for technical or other purposes, would certainly have taken advantage of the *Wolverine* lift, but they had set out on a canoe venture, and any alternative was bound to be a letdown. On the other hand, riding the hazardous sea meant delay, and delay meant possible freeze-up of the inland waters.

The layover between open water and freeze-up is usually about two weeks long. And although the change from canoe travel to toboggan or sled is not difficult, this seasonal, transitional mode of travel calls for clothes, equipment, and know-how. Camping in the wilderness under winter conditions is far from perilous, but it does require winter procedure. (See "Winter Camping and Travel" in my book, *The New Way of the Wilderness*, published by The Macmillan Company.)

The moral and physical lift Sevareid and Port received at Norway House, a wilderness settlement at the upper end of Lake Winnipeg, was a great help. They managed to travel part of the way in the wake of a post manager and two Indians in a canoe. Finally, they were again on their own. Their route became uncertain. The last lap into York Factory was a desperate striking out; they ate cold beans, suffered from the chill of late fall, and nagged each other until they came to blows—but this was no more than an effect of simple bush psychosis. Yet both knew that their success—perhaps their very lives—depended on each other, so they went on.

York Factory had originally been proposed as the railroad terminal to Hudson Bay, but later Churchill was chosen. The change left York Factory 90 miles from the railroad. Here on the shore at York Factory, Sevareid and Post abandoned their canoe and other needless equipment, and, with the aid of some Indians, managed to work their way to the railroad and eventually back to Minneapolis.

Today, whenever I hear Eric Sevareid's sound journalistic comments on the human struggles of the world, I like to think that his broad outlook stems in part from this extraordinary canoe journey that he and Walter Port took early in life.

The Oberholtzer–Magie Journey

The canoe journey by Ernest C. Oberholtzer and his Indian companion, Billy Magie, in 1912 from The Pas, Manitoba, to the upper end of Nueltin Lake, down the Thlewiaza River to Hudson Bay, up the swift Hayes River to Lake Winnipeg, and down the length of Lake Winnipeg to the town of Gimli on the south shore, in a single season, has special significance for the present-day canoe voyager. The journey was made by paddle.

As far as I have been able to determine, Oberholtzer was the first white man to visit Nueltin Lake since 1770, when the noted explorer, Samuel Hearne, reached its shores. A large part of the route had not been charted in 1912.

This journey was made without reliance on the country for subsistence—which in itself makes the account unusually interesting—and, Mr. Oberholtzer told me, he and his partner had to make five trips over the portages at the start.

In a wilderness of game animals, five portages may seem a needless ordeal. But here was a journey into an area where sustenance otherwise depended upon the movement of the caribou. It is generally better to travel slowly and be self-sustaining than to speed along with uncertainty. (Also, Oberholtzer is a characteristically thoughtful man with strong feelings about wildlife preservation. His contribution toward formulating the Quetico-Superior program—saving the border area from commercial ravage—has made him a noted conservation figure in the annals of this cause.)

One cannot even imagine the labor entailed in five trips over the portages without knowing about the Little Lakes country. Between the Cochrane River and Theitaga Lake, portages become a job of clawing and scrambling over precipitous eskers, and virtually sliding down their steep slopes on the other side. Portage trails were difficult to find; caribou trails ran everywhere to confuse the route, crisscrossing endlessly, dividing the earth into an infinite number of mosaic patterns.

The Indian, Billy Magie, was fifty years old when he made the trip; Oberholtzer was just a few years out of college. Six months of travel on the Rainy Lake watershed had prepared Oberholtzer for the long journey to Nueltin Lake. Whatever experience he lacked was complemented by Magie's half century of living as a forest Indian, an invaluable combination of ages and experiences.

They left The Pas, Manitoba, on the Saskatchewan River, June 26, 1912, in an 18-foot Chestnut canoe—a rugged craft of good depth and wide beam. Three days later, they were at Cumberland House, Hudson Bay Post. The Post, established by Samuel Hearne in 1773, prospered immediately, and has been successful ever since. A week later, Oberholtzer and Magie arrived at Beaver Lake, and in another five days reached Pelican Narrows. Passing over the famous Frog Portage to the Churchill River and into Reindeer River, they reached the south end of Reindeer Lake on July 19.

The complexity of Reindeer Lake, with its many islands, points, and indentations of water, can readily be seen on an aerial map, but no impression can equal actual canoe travel on it. This is one of the truly impressive lakes of the North. The intrepid explorer, David Thompson, mapped it in 1798, wintering on the west shore. The lake is about a hundred and forty miles long, but its meandering canoe route is about a hundred and seventy miles. Although the lake has numerous islands, and is broken by a variety of headlands, large open-water stretches make it hazardous travel with a canoe in winds even of the common, brisk variety—to say nothing of the sudden blows that bear down unheralded on the lake. It is a clear-water lake, with trout and whitefish. Oberholtzer and Magie managed the long haul through the lake in about nine days, arriving at Brochet Hudson Bay Post at the upper end on July 27. Twelve days later, they reached Theitaga Lake, where they entered the Thlewiaza River, leading into Nueltin Lake (Nu-thel-tin-tu-eh).

This was a world uncharted. The Thlewiaza River flows out of Nueltin Lake, and ultimately finds its way into Hudson Bay. But where in this maze of a hundred miles or more of islands, points, and bays was the river? They followed the east shore in all of its many indentations, for here was water where two men in a canoe could wander hopelessly. The river might be neatly tucked away behind a headland, invisible from a short distance. They managed to avoid one huge bay, which Magie thought looked as large as Rainy Lake, by climbing a high summit, and concluding with some hesitancy that the outlet of the lake could hardly be found among those lofty ridges.

The search through every indentation, however, paid off, and one day they found themselves entering the

Thlewiaza River. A long journey still awaited them, but the route from here on followed a more sensible pattern. Through the eskers and Little Lakes, through Reindeer and Nueltin Lake, the pattern of travel had been infinitely complex, testing spirit and resourcefulness, bringing the sun down each day on two apprehensive but determined canoe voyagers.

Nueltin Lake consists of a series of five expansive water areas with narrow passages between. Swift water connects the expanses at some of these narrows. When the lake seems about to end, a water doorway opens at one of the narrows, displaying another disconcerting fresh-water sea, shattering the promise of escape into the Thlewiaza River. They spent two weeks on Nueltin.

Barren-ground caribou, traveling upwind by the thousands, were continuously visible from morning to night. Timber wolves, their attention entirely on the caribou, paid little heed to the canoe voyagers. The wolves, an integral part of the caribou herds, were ever ready to pounce on a weak straggler. Thus the herd is kept vigorous.

It is a strange world, this "land of Little Sticks," where the forests are gradually merging into the great arctic prairie. It was September before they had traversed the Thlewiaza from Nueltin to the river's end. Here the Thlewiaza River empties into the salt water where the Atlantic has elbowed its way into the eastern half of the continent to form the vast reaches of Hudson Bay and James Bay.

Portage trails had been few from Nueltin through Theitaga to the sea. Rivers were extremely rough, with unpredictable, circuitous rapids. All this white water, which had to be examined from the shore, found its way through glacial debris with boulders as big as houses, making the lining of the canoe through the river with ropes a continually uncertain procedure. The water level was low, creating long stretches where rapids could not be run, and making the route seem interminable. There was frequent wading to get past sections of the river where neither lining nor paddling was practical, and the canoe had to be laboriously dragged through these circuitous shallows.

September in the North is a time when the winds rile the big waters to the point of madness. At the mouth of the Thlewiaza River on Hudson Bay, Oberholtzer and Magie came upon an Eskimo family. The Eskimos owned a small, crude sailboat, and agreed to transport the voyagers to Churchill, where they arrived September 19. This is a trying coast to travel with a canoe or other small craft in the autumn storms, because at low tide, with the very low, sloping shores, you are out from 2 to 12 miles in a great salt-water sea.

At Churchill, Oberholtzer and Magie replenished their supplies, and continued by canoe down the coast of Hudson Bay to York Factory to enter the Hayes River for the upstream voyage, and then through tributary lakes to the upper end of Lake Winnipeg.

They reached the north end of Lake Winnipeg on October 19, hoping to catch a steamer to the south end of the lake. To their dismay, the last boat of the season had left. This called for a trip of several hundred additional miles by canoe at the beginning of winter, and nothing remained but to get about their task—unless they wanted to winter here, or wait for the freeze-up and travel by dog team.

At this time of year in these higher latitudes, snow and

sleet storms make travel on reef-ridden Lake Winnipeg a great hazard. An upset in the heavy sea during the warm season may be tragic; in the icy waters of October and November, an upset is almost certain to be so. Reefs projecting from the shore make it necessary to paddle far out into the heavy breakers to avoid foundering on these shoals.

This was the prospect they faced for 18 days and 300 miles. Oberholtzer told me that they encountered much snow, ice, and heavy winds. On the evening of November 5, they managed to cross the lower part of the lake, and came to the end of their journey at the little Icelandic settlement of Gimli.

Here was warmth, and here was carefully prepared food, spread on checkered tablecloths. Ice along the edges of the lake was breaking loose, and churning about by the breakers, the sea fighting its encroaching winter bonds. But within it was cozy for the travelers. Victory was theirs.

The transition from months of adventure to a passive existence is not easy. Routine comfort and living, by comparison to the great adventure, seem without purpose. Gradually, you begin thinking about the back trail. Even the snow-and-sleet-blown icy camps along the east shore of Lake Winnipeg, the uncertain days along Nueltin Lake, the scramble over the eskers, were closer to the vital elements of living.

Gradually, as the months pass, you emerge from your frustration. The plan for a new adventure begins to form in your mind. Day by day it gains force. Then one day, a canoe, a pack train, a dog team, are again poised on a remote frontier.

8 GOING ALONE

MAN is a gregarious being, and he is constantly reminded of it. Yet his most profound moments generally occur when he is by himself.

Few of us have ventured very far into the wilderness alone, and we are not without loneliness when we do. I have paddled dolefully away from the few Indian shelters around a far north Hudson Bay Post, and labored in solitude for weeks over portage and water routes, when a simple invitation would have secured a pleasant companion for the bow or stern of my canoe.

Why, then, do we go alone?

My experience has convinced me that, to feel profoundly the enchantment of the wilderness, we must go in complete solitude at one time or another. A journey with others has a separate set of values of unquestionable enjoyment, but it should never be categorically compared to travel alone. In the lone journey you live closer to the nerve ends of feeling, where subjective response to the world around you becomes complete—objective response having been lost in the very intimacy of your natural existence. With companions, you saw your world with the eyes of aliens seeking novelty. Alone, you become a part of that phenomenon which was novelty, an integration that only the lone traveler ever experiences.

Possibly, it is best to be thrown upon the lone venture by accident or circumstance, rather than to plan it deliberately—the temptation to abandon the idea at the last moment is too great.

When the season for canoe travel is upon you, and your partner has backed out, either you delay departure and look for a replacement, or you go alone. You may find a willing companion at an outpost—or attach yourself to a group of Indians, or some agent such as a post manager, or a missionary who is traveling into the interior toward a fixed destination. This "barnacle" attachment does not always prove satisfactory, however. The others, generally, are heading in a direction off your itinerary, and one fine morning you will simply drift off on a diverting canoe route, wave goodbye, and lose yourself over a more promising horizon of adventure.

There are, of course, mixed emotions, but you have a great sense of relief. For you have been traveling by the methods of others; camping and eating their way, not yours; rising early on cold, wet mornings when you would rather sleep; laboring cooperatively with heavy, bulky equipment not up to your own standards.

In a way, you will miss the stories around the campfire, the boasts, the ribbing, the excitement and turmoil of portage trails and camps. Most of all, you may miss one individual who is an anthology of wilderness experience —possibly with a unique philosophy of life. But even his stories become tedious in time.

Alone at your very next camp, with a deep sense of escape and freedom, you prepare the foods you want in your own way, pitch your tent on the site you choose. Alone, you maintain a capricious schedule, traveling hard when

Why Do We Go Alone?

you feel like it, quietly contemplating the scene when you are so inclined.

As the solitary days draw on, much of the loneliness passes. Wildlife springs magically into view as you control every sound of your own movements and those connected with your craft, equipment, and its operation.

You have a great feeling of well-being, a growing sense of infallibility. You seem not to err in anything. There is an unconscious awareness but no feeling of apprehension that now each step over a portage trail has become a bit more precise, that your individual acts of swinging an ax and lifting a canoe are less haphazard. You are only dimly aware of the consequences that a false move entails; ex-

pertness by reflex action is brought into every act. Unconsciously, you are methodical, accurate, careful. Much of this comes by being freed from the diversion of companionship.

Daylight, especially bright sun, dispels most loneliness, and so does the deep darkness when a cheerful fire is going, and the evening meal is over. But the in-between, the dying day, invariably brings on melancholy; you crave companionship. After dusk, the campfire dispels loneliness by losing you in reflective thought, or the sounds of the night move in to entrance.

In the tent, the white-light luxury of a mantle lantern offers the exquisite pleasure of lying in a down robe to read—a pleasure intensified when rain patters on the tent roof. The mantle lantern is really my only extravagant item of equipment. On chilly evenings and mornings, the heat from this lantern raises the temperature of the tent about twenty degrees. An improvised plate at the crown of the lantern permits heating but not cooking of food. Sometimes the lantern seems like a dull and needless care on the portage trails, but its virtues have certainly outweighed its evils on the solitary journey.

Only those who awake at dawn alone in a wilderness can know the thoughts and feelings of the solitary traveler. At the first sign of wakefulness, you are seized with a sudden realization that for many hours you have lain unconscious and isolated in the wilderness. It is a strange and rare experience.

The song of a white-throated sparrow, just faintly audible at dawn, rising and falling in modulation from the near fringes of the coniferous forest; the rhythmic slap of waves on the shore; the gentle breeze buffeting the sides of your tent—these and many of the effects which are normally obscured by the presence of other people now become vivid parts of your surroundings. Even the tiny silhouette of an insect crawling up the steep incline of your shelter roof becomes fascinating; you wonder if he has a destination, or if it is only—as with most of us—the climb that is really important. A duck quacking in the nearby bay, the wild call of a loon out on the lake, seem to lend increasing mystery and enchantment to these first waking moments.

Warmth of the down sleeping robe gives a feeling of security in the chill of the fall morning. But you boldly throw aside the covers, and examine the wild scene of an

approaching new day. A large red solar disk is creeping up
from the horizon, not bringing much warmth yet, perhaps, but promising. There, wet and uninspiring, lies the
drab heap of ashes from the evening's extinguished fire. A
red squirrel chatters in spasms from a nearby limb as he
suddenly discovers you. You speak to him to hear the
sound of your own voice, and find it shocking in the early
quiet. Chickadees flit about with incredible friendly confidence. The next move is to build a fire, and you get at it.
Once you have poured the first cup of coffee before the
warmth of an early, open fire, the new day begins.

Senses actually seem to be made sharper by the concentration effected in solo travel. There is less diversion, less
distraction—a clearing of the atmosphere for a sharper
response. One develops a keener ear for sound, a more

The Wild Call of a Loon

perceptive eye for movement. A favorite pastime when alone is to scan the far shore with a pair of compact binoculars in search of wildlife. You do not "panoram." This brings few results. You practice the Indian's method: With the naked eye, he isolates a segment of distant shore, and scrutinizes it carefully, then shifts his vision to another small aggregate area. He is not looking for a distinct animal form. He watches particular rocks, the semblance of a piece of driftwood, vague shadows—any indistinguishable formations on water or shore. If the pattern changes shape at all—if a boulder or what seemed a partly submerged deadhead alters its position ever so slightly—his focus acts upon the center of that change. In time something may take form, be actuated into a living thing. What at first

A Red Squirrel Chatters in Spasms

Chickadees Flit About with Incredible Friendly Confidence

looked like a boulder or deadhead may turn out to be a bear, a moose, a caribou, a lynx, or some lesser creature.

One morning as you paddle up a small tributary of a river, you may come upon several woodland caribou splashing across the stream. They stop, stare for a few seconds, then slowly saunter off into the forest. Near a cataract, you may slip into the rushes of a backwater, and watch a bear fishing. The noise of the water and his concentration on his prey let you go unnoticed. Another time, you may see several otter at play on a slide. These are sights that have been seen many times, of course, by parties traveling extensively in the wilderness, but they do not have the intensified interest and meaning allowed the lone traveler. Life of the solitary man by its very nature becomes subjective. You are not the intruder; you feel yourself an integral part of the composite natural scheme.

A simpler, more elemental approach is thus made to all

things. It has been said that we are constantly acting in the presence of others. This dramatic tension does not exist when you are alone. If you choose to eat out of the frying pan and drink out of the teapot—be your own guest. I must confess that I like more primordial ways when I am alone. I prefer a skewered fish that has been propped before a fire and baked, eaten with my hands, to a fried fish served on a plate, eaten with a knife and fork. You wash your hands, rinse the teapot—all without re- dundancies. There is pure art in watching a lone Indian travel and camp with a tea pail, knife, fishline, rifle, rabbit- skin blanket, canoe, and paddle. He sleeps in his blanket under the canoe, lives off the country, performing each act with incredible simplicity. I have experienced great pleasure in leaving things behind as I continued over an arduous route. In the wilderness, domestic austerity can become luxury. A set of nesting pails gets reduced from

What Looks Like a Deadhead May Turn Out to Be a Moose

four to two or even one. A change of clothing is left hanging on a tree for some Indian or other traveler, whose own may be worn to shreds. If, with a little patching, the trousers you have on are good for the remaining few hundred miles of your travel, why carry an extra pair? These are the concepts that become more apparent on solo trips, because you alone must tote and care for every last item.

Somehow, Indians have great respect for a white man traveling alone. They themselves know the rigors and loneliness of the long trail. Traveling alone thus marks you with a badge of distinction in their eyes. An Indian canoe party in a remote area may drift on by if they see two or more white men camping. If they find a lone camper, they will invariably stop and chat, share their supplies, or yours.

Paddling a canoe alone creates no problem. Equipment packed around the bow seat counterbalances the weight of a stern paddler in average water. Where the canoe is paddled without counterbalancing equipment, as it may be when fishing in a brisk wind, or in running rapids, a position at the center of the canoe will have to be taken. (The use of rocks for counterbalance is a risky practice where the water is rough enough for a possible upset. Rather use a clump of dry log which will float. Rocks lodged in one end can set an overturned canoe on end.)

A popular notion is that a very small canoe is needed for one man and his outfit. This will hold true for a trapper moving in and out of small lakes and streams requiring much portaging and little water travel. On extended canoe journeys, short canoes, as I have pointed out, ride deep and paddle sluggishly. Each foot of canoe-length gained

Woodland Caribou Splashing Across a Stream

raises the canoe measurably higher out of the water, increases the canoeist's capacity for running through heavy
seas and rapids—but especially facilitates rapid movement
over long stretches of water.

Once you have made your solitary journey into the
wilderness, you will have discovered a new dimension in
living—an increased capacity to absorb the spirit of the
wilderness—and you will undoubtedly be unable to resist
the lure of going alone again and again.

9 RECOLLECTIONS AND INDIANS

WHEN I look back over almost half a century of canoe travel, trails seem numerous, intricate, long, and—often enough—rugged. Yet, as I observe the topography of North America, I realize that one lifetime can cover but a limited part of the great network of existing waterways. We are apt to become a bit vainglorious in our boast of long travel by canoe until we recognize the insignificant scope of travel a single individual can accomplish even in a half-century of consistent effort. But, fortunately, this always leaves untraveled trails for the future.

"What do you consider your most impressive wilderness experience?" is a question often posed. There can be no illusion about this for me. I must seriously hark back to the impressions at age eighteen, when I made my first significant canoe voyage—three and one-half months—traveling by canoe until freeze-up, and coming out by sled. Later in life I have experienced a nostalgic passion to recapture the thrill of the wilderness as I felt it at eighteen.

It isn't quite accurate to refer to my earlier days of canoe travel in the wilderness as simply canoe trips. Commercial employment in the cities was at that time only a means to an end. The end was to get a grubstake in order to remain in the wilderness for an indefinite period. While my first venture into the canoe country of the North lasted three and one-half months, most subsequent returns to the wilderness were longer—as long as I could afford. Trip followed trip, in no set pattern. Season overlapped season; sometimes a canoe was hauled in by dog sled or toboggan, or a toboggan was hauled in by canoe.

When traveling by canoe, hauling a toboggan or sledge, dogs were released and allowed to run along the shore. They swam across narrows or were hauled by canoe if a span of water was so wide that it risked losing them. When they followed the shore, I could hear their wolfish vocalizing off in the distance, running down some hapless forest creature, or getting into an occasional fight among themselves, or while confronting a forest creature. Somehow, a little worse for wear, and on occasion licking their bloody chops or their own wounds, they generally showed up on the next portage trail, hungry, tongues protruding, and displaying great, wag-tail happiness over the reunion with me.

It may not be wise to regard with too much nostalgia what happened early in life. There is a vast wilderness still remaining to challenge present and future canoe voyagers. Yet we can have no illusions. Something of isolation and remoteness is surely lost today. Early in the century, when there was no radio or plane contact with the outside world, canoe travelers reaching a Hudson Bay outpost provided the post manager with a valuable source of news from the "outside." Arrivals at the post were new associations for the factors and a capital relief for the canoe voyager. The guest was king. If he departed in less than several days, the post manager was keenly disappointed. Talk lasted far into the night—small talk and big talk about wilderness equipment and travel methods, personal matters, and world problems—the hunger for human relationship and individual expression in a lone and challenging land.

In the earlier period, as a guest of a Hudson Bay factor, I ate fresh caribou steak, steamed rice, and brown-sugar-cinnamon-topped cobbler made with reconstituted dry apples. It would have been insulting to suggest that I pay for these excellent meals. A few years ago on a dog sled trip, I stopped at a Hudson Bay post in midwinter, ate choice beef T-bone steaks, fresh frozen vegetables, with fresh frozen strawberry shortcake for dessert. I sat at a table with two female schoolteachers from Iowa, who had flown in for a vacation. When I departed, I paid my bill at tourist rates.

This is no deviation from hospitality by the Hudson's Bay Company—it is a change in the times and travel facilities. HBC outposts would be far in the red were they to operate now on the old basis. Access by plane is too easy. The reverse of earlier times, outside world news is now given by the HBC factors up to date by radio to the canoe voyager—unless he happens to be carrying a radio with him in the canoe. And if the canoe party members wish to "call home," they can do so by HBC two-way radio. There are, of course, some variations to this theme of straight commercialism in the more remote outposts, where HBC factors seldom see people from the outside, and are able to accept the voyager as a family guest. It is, naturally, just a matter of common sense and circumstance.

I don't mean to be sentimental about this change. Remote areas of North American canoe country are still sufficiently isolated to offer the true flavor of wilderness romance. Some things, of course, are lost, such as the achievement of reaching a remote area unattainable except by the rigors of hard travel by canoe and over portage trails. Now, all can be reached by anyone having the price of a chartered flight. A great deal is gone, but much is left.

I miss the familiar tub of coiled rope tobacco that customarily sat on the floor in front of the counter at the Hudson Bay posts. Also, I miss the aromatic attic loft of the HBC post with its numerous pairs of fragrant, smoke-tanned moccasins. Indian moccasins can still be found—but it is a bit disillusioning to learn that bundles of moose hides are now being flown to tanneries for commercial treatment. The fact that it took Indians weeks on end to tan a moose or caribou hide, and that they were paid little for their work, certainly offers economic logic, if not solace for those of us who mourn a vanishing art and craft. However, some Indians have discovered commercially tanned hides to be unsatisfactory for moccasins and other wilderness uses, and have now gone back to tanning the hides themselves.

I miss those years of canoe travel with Indians when only paddles were used—the outboard motor's raucous noise and odor yet unknown. There was a deep peace in the rhythmic dip of paddles and a special thrill when shouts of gaiety echoed against the forest wall. The outboard motor has usurped much of this, but the Indians still do paddle their canoes.

If you are an Indian in spirit (this takes time), you will find Indians a happy people—an incredibly wonderful people. Spend a few days with a family of Indians while they are smoking and drying the meat of a moose on a wilderness island. You will discover domestic bliss—a togetherness unexcelled in most human relations. Do them a good turn at a time when they need it most, and you will discover a response as deep as can be found in any other society.

At one time, nearing the end of a long journey, I came across a tiny cache of dried moose meat hanging over a river along my route. The cache was so small that I was prompted to tie all my excess provisions to it. Some days later, nearing a reservation, I stopped to buy a tanned moose hide, but found that most of the Indians had gone off to the north, beyond the cache, leaving behind only some extremely old and feeble Indians. To them, I expressed my keen disappointment at not getting a moose hide. When I reached the CNR Railroad, I stopped for a few days at a fishing camp. One evening there was a knock at the door of the camp's lodge. (Only Indians knocked here before they came in.)

"There is an Indian out here who wants to see 'The Man from English River,'" a guest called out. I had just come through a part of the English River on my trip from the north.

In the darkness outside, the Indian handed me a rolled-up, Indian-tanned moose hide, gently tapped my arm, and with a warm smile, departed without a word. Later I learned that he had traveled days to offer this token of thanks for the food I had left at the cache.

Somewhat abashed, I followed him to the shore where he was to spend the night in a rabbitskin blanket under his canoe. I wanted to pay for the hide, but felt this was a touchy business. It was at the suggestion of the camp's manager that I finally settled the matter by sending a gift of luxury-type provisions back to the Indians at the reservation. Money would have been insulting.

Some years later, on a trip with a companion through this same region, I brought along an extra packsack of food. When we reached the Indian reservation, we learned that the Indians were a short distance north, camped on an island to avoid the last onslaught of the insect season. We left some food with the old people at the reservation, and toward evening reached the island. Although it was not the scheduled period for potlatches, our arrival brought on a potlatch of the first order. At daylight, after all-night feasting, my partner and I headed north. Two husky Indian lads followed in another canoe, and carried our equipment and canoe across the portage at the upper end of the lake. They were genuinely unhappy to leave us. We shook hands, smiled, and uttered a mixture of Cree and English.

But relations between white men and Indians are not always amicable. Too many white men carry irrational prejudices, and Indians are often exceptionally sensitive people. Early in the fall of 1962 when I reached Sioux Lookout, Ontario, Canada, I arrived in a carryall with a canoe and equipment. As I unlashed the canoe from the top of the carryall for further shipment by rail, an elderly Indian of magnificent physical build watched me preparing to unload the canoe. He made no overtures to assist me until I looked his way and smiled. Then, he fairly leaped into action. He explained that he did not, at first, wish to offer help because "Sometimes, Indians are told to mind their own business."

News travels incredibly fast on the "grapevine tele-graph" of canoe country. Among the Indians, you are named and classified as to your character with such dis-patch that you almost wonder if there actually is some telepathic communication among them. They, like the rest of us, respect ability and courage. While they are realistic and receptive where generosity is concerned, you do not gain dignity or advantage by throwing around your financial or material weight.

On a canoe trip through a section east of Lake Winnipeg, I had been told that because of an unpleasant incident, some of the Indians were not very helpful, either in acting as guides, or giving information for travel over the watershed—a rather devious route I had planned to take through small and uncertain water. I encountered the first few Indians of that region at a short portage, where they seemed to be in a semipermanent camp. My meeting with them seemed quite casual, until I heard a man's moans coming from one of the tents.

"What's wrong with him?" I asked.

"*Akosew, osikowin.*" ("Sick, hurt.")

This was the reason for their semipermanent camp.

Several days earlier, the enfeebled Indian had cut his thigh with an ax that had accidentally flipped out of his hand. The cut was not in a vital area, but an infection had developed that seemed to be steering him directly and rapidly toward the Happy Hunting Grounds. His leg had swelled to twice its size.

A large yellow bulge appeared in the region of the cut. This might in time have burst to release the infection— except that, from all appearances, this man did not have time to spare. Whatever the consequences, I felt compelled at the moment to do what I could; and with my sheath knife, I boldly opened the locus of infection to treat the wound.

A high fever persisted into the night. I played nurse and doctor without sleep. At this point, had the Indian died, it is doubtful from the attitude of the others that *North American Canoe Country* would ever have been written.

In the early morning hours, a heavy thunderhead rolled

up, and it rained violently. Suddenly, my patient, who had been half-delirious up to this time, turned his head toward me and mumbled, *"Kimewun"* ("rain"). Feebly, he asked who I was—how I got there. My relief soared. The crisis had passed.

"Muskikeweyinew" ("doctor"), I lied.

Late that morning, a small flotilla of canoes with a motley group of Indians came into camp—mostly women with youngsters, but also two adult men. Everyone started chattering excitedly about the sick Indian and the *muskikeweyinew.*

The closest translation of the confused discussion was, "A miracle has been performed." The patient was propped against a tree, sitting up, taking nourishment, while chlorazene antiseptic solution flowed through his wound from a birchbark funnel tied to a tree trunk.

As the day wore on, Indian women washed, mended, and resmoked my moccasins—their token of thanks.

Another confusion of Cree controversy arose when I prepared to leave. With my limited understanding of Cree, I gathered that the women were trying to pressure their men into taking me over the watershed. Once the idea sparked, it seemed to catch fire with everybody. In the two days that followed, I could not lift a finger. I sat midship in the canoe with more protocol and ceremony than ever did Mr. Simpson, early Governor of the Hudson's Bay Company.

When I use the term "Indians," I am including Eskimos. Something in the ethnic makeup of the Eskimo responds more readily to the white man's industrial psychosis than the Indian. Yet, among the older Eskimos I find the theme much the same, "Not like long ago." Both Indian and Eskimo are easily victimized—who isn't?—by

the fruits of industrialism. Nevertheless, there is a strong
disinclination on the part of both to play the sedulous ape
to the white man's ways. The popular notion that Indians
are lazy derives from a confused concept. They are in no
sense lazy; they have the ability to relax and not develop
white man's ulcers. The white man's year-round employment enslavement seems foolish and needless to them—a
point of view growing in popularity among rational individuals of all races.

Many times you ask yourself, "Why travel in the wilderness?" Is it worthwhile? When I see the grim realities
even in the normal abuse of equipment, the "why" keeps
repeating itself. Is it illusory and deceptive that you recall
more vividly the pleasures? In the final analysis, it is un-
thinkable for you to give up wilderness travel, even with
its rugged demands.

Equipment depreciated from rough service suggests no
small measure of adversity. We need have no illusions:
the sweat-soaked, stained tumpline and packsack head-
straps are clear evidence of having tugged heavy loads
over brush-covered portage trails that were scarcely more
than uncertain general directions over an obstacle course.
Neither have you forgotten the portage trails where you
dragged canoe and equipment up steep inclines of slippery, rocky slopes with tracking lines; nor where the only
means of crossing a river with a canoe on one's back was
to fell a giant tree across a gorge, and hope to maintain
balance on this precarious bridge—a roaring cataract
below challenging and threatening every step. You are
aware of the crystal-clear waters that allow you to look a
fish in the eye at 15 feet, but you do not forget the tea
water taken from the drainage of a bog, brown as burnt

umber, or the water you had to screen through a cloth after a heavy rain in the clay belt.

Also never vague in memory are the insects so dense on the rivers of the tundra and the northern forest belt; you viewed your world for weeks only through the soft focus of a headnet, and paddled the canoe with hands encased in hot, sweaty, leather gloves.

The life involved, however, is not entirely grim. Pain is not, after all, the normal state. Scars are not too numerous. And nothing can compare with waking in a tent before daylight and watching the earliest glimmer of light break slowly across the forest wilderness. No cup of coffee rivals that which you drink on the rockbound shore of a wilderness lake, before a wood fire that is competing with the first rays of dawn.

If there is a laborious tugging on the sweat-soaked pack straps; so too, is there a half moon in night's magic silence just tipping the opposite, spruce-covered shore; or so are there northern lights flashing great veils of fluorescence. And if this were not enough for momentary fulfillment, the complement of a loon calling and echoing across the peaceful water a mile away is bound to leave you entranced.

You can make a discriminating choice of the proper month for canoe travel, but uncanny though it may seem, you do manage to cope with each problem in all kinds of weather and circumstances. Consequently, there comes a time when you can virtually disregard the various encroachments upon your wilderness comfort—a day or two without food, successive days of rain, being windbound upon an island, the onslaught of heat and insects—these, and a hundred others, are not sufficient to dissuade or dishearten.

10 ORGANIZED YOUTH CAMP CANOEING

ORGANIZED youth camps for both boys and girls are a vast enterprise. Seven to ten million youngsters go to camp each summer in Canada and the United States. A large number of these camps are in areas where canoe travel is an important part of the program.

Safety takes priority, of course, where youngsters are concerned. As director of wilderness activity programs in both boys' and girls' camps for more than ten years, I found that safety was best accomplished by training campers to be self-sufficient and to cope with each emergency—not simply teaching them caution or giving warnings. The least regimentation develops the greatest resourcefulness—the best safety and training factor.

The initial requirement is that the youngsters be able to swim at least 200 yards. But they must understand that they should never swim away from their craft in an upset.

The next step is to teach them how to make a recovery in the event of an upset with all equipment packed in waterproof containers so it will float. The youngsters are put through a routine series of upsets and recoveries, first in shallow water, then in deep water, under adequate supervision by life guards.

One recovery method of an upset canoe and its occupants is made with the aid of two other crewmen in an upright canoe. The two in the water hold onto the swamped canoe for support. As the rescue canoe nears the upset canoe, the two members in the water roll the swamped canoe right side up, and both go to the far end of the swamped canoe, pulling this end slightly down into the water. This raises the opposite end, which is grasped by the members in the upright canoe, then drawn in this upright position only a few feet over the gunwale. The swamped canoe is then rolled over, so that it is upside down, and drawn over the upright canoe to the middle of the swamped canoe. The process is not dangerous because the rescued canoe has an outrigger effect upon the upright canoe, and stabilizes it. The rescued canoe remains there until drained, and is then rolled right side up and slipped back into the water.

The foregoing method applies only to wood and wood-and-canvas canoes. Because the buoyancy of aluminum canoes is concentrated entirely in the air or Styrofoam compartments at each end, these ends on an upset canoe cannot be pulled down into the water by the swimmers as can the open ends of canvas canoes. For this reason, the aluminum canoe should first be rolled on its side during recovery. Then, when the swamped members in the water pull down on one end, the curvature of the canoe will allow the bow to rise high enough for the rescuers to draw the upset canoe over the upright canoe, where they can turn it upside down to drain in the same manner as the canvas canoe. (This side recovery method also applies to Fiberglas, plastic canoes.)

In the meantime, those in the water have been supporting themselves by gently holding onto the rescue canoe.

When the upset canoe has been returned to the water, its crewmen enter it one at a time, face down, using a flutter kick as in swimming. While one enters the canoe at the middle thwart, the other should counterbalance the canoe by holding onto the gunwale at the opposite side. By grasping a thwart, the member draws his body over the canoe until his buttocks just clear the gunwales. At this point, he rolls over, dropping seat first into the bottom of the canoe. When the first man is in the canoe, he takes a position on the floor, well into the bilge at the opposite side of the canoe from where the second is to enter, thus giving counterbalance. Lost paddles and equipment can be recovered by the rescue canoe team, but preferably for training purposes the swamped members should make this equipment recovery by getting to their knees in the canoe and "swimming" it to the floating items.

It is well to consider that on canoe trips, later in life, no second canoe is likely to be present for recovery. Recovery knowledge of a single canoe by the upset occupants is thus important in the organized camp program.

An aluminum canoe, when upset, can be tossed upright, almost emptied, in deep water. The swamped members first roll the canoe over, bottom up. (Canvas canoes always float upside down.) An aluminum canoe will always right itself, and so will most Fiberglas, plastic canoes. The plan is for the canoeists to swim under the inverted canoe, one taking hold of the front thwart, the other the rear thwart. The canoe is then tipped sidewise, just slightly, to allow air to flow under the inverted canoe and thus avoid a vacuum. At a signal, both throw the canoe upward and over. This, naturally, drives the swimmers down into the water. They should return to the surface as quickly as possible with a rapid swimming stroke toward the lee side of the canoe, so that the wind will not blow the canoe too far away for them to retrieve it quickly. The wind can blow a canoe faster than swimmers can catch up to it.

Emptying an aluminum canoe can also be done by one individual if he happens to be alone, by taking his position at the center thwart and performing the operation described for two individuals. Whatever water remains in the canoe can be sponged out with a garment or bailed out with cupped hands. Canoes heavier than aluminum may not be recovered by the throw-over method. These should be splashed out by a rhythmic rocking of the canoe, until one person can get in. With cupped hands additional water is bailed out, after which the second crewman gets in.

When campers have accomplished this recovery well enough so that parents have reasonable assurance of getting their youngsters back alive at the end of the season, they should go on a "local" canoe trip. By that time, the campers will also have learned something about pitching tents, cooking over an open fire, using a compass; camp sanitation, order, cleanliness, cooperation, and general safety.

On the conclusion of the local trip through rivers and lakes nearby—a trip generally lasting about three days— the counselor-guide in charge of the party usually knows if youngsters are qualified to go on a major wilderness trip. Merit badges for accomplishment—a canoe paddle with the name and the major trip boldly lettered on the blade by a sign painter, for example—become highly cherished mementos through adulthood.

Most camping areas, especially those in the deep forests

of the North, generally do not have sufficient space for large canoe groups to pitch all of their tents. The ideal number of campers for each group is seven or eight with three canoes and three tents. The capacity of the canoes will allow one or two campers to ride as "dead weight," and if one of the six paddlers happens to be indisposed for some reason, you have a substitute paddler.

Several small tents, each sheltering only two or three campers, are better than big, unwieldy tents accommodating larger groups. The small groups thus get individual tent-pitching training. Cooking and eating are best done, perhaps, as a full group, since it lends more festivity to the occasion, although some small group or individual cooking should be practiced at times.

It is important when traveling that canoes remain together, at least within vision or easy hailing distance of one another. Canoes falling behind the full vision of the counselor-guide are apt to become an increasing hazard. One counselor-guide in organized youth camps should be an adult, to avoid negligence suits of a technical nature against the camp in the event of an accident.

Two schools of thought prevail regarding teaching methods for wilderness canoe trips—one where the camper is taught in camp, the other as he proceeds on a trip. I have found that the first creates the best results if the instruction is enjoyable enough not to be considered tedious classroom teaching. On a trip, have every camper participate, so that he will acquire field knowledge and will feel important.

While the summer camp season seems ample to put over a canoe program, the fact is that the time allotted to each activity does not allow thoroughness. As a director, I sought every possible shortcut to quick learning. One of these was to watch carefully to see that a camper practiced proper procedure instead of practicing his mistakes. I am not being facetious. Unknowingly, campers have actually performed chronic errors with diligent practice for whole seasons. One of these perpetuated errors is extending the blade of the paddle too far from the canoe. A paddle extended thus does little more than swerve a canoe from side to side. Improvement time was cut from days to hours when, by exaggeration, I suggested that the camper paddle *under* the canoe, not away from it. This brought quizzical stares and strange paddling antics, but the final result was that the stroke was pulled in near, and even slightly under, the canoe, eliminating most of the swerving.

Keep canoe strokes few and simple at the start to avoid confusion and to inspire confidence. Initiate the pitch stroke for propelling the canoe on its forward course, the quarter-sweep to get turned around, with instructions in how to backwater to avoid collisions. While I do not like to suggest a stroke that must be abandoned later, the "J" stroke is admittedly easier for youngsters to master at the start. If used, it should be discontinued and the pitch stroke adopted as soon as possible. (See Chapter 4 for performance of these strokes. See *The New Way of the Wilderness*, The Macmillan Company, for detailed camp procedure.)

11 THE CANOE OUTFITTER

CANOE outfitting is a well-established business. All you need to take with you are your clothes, toilet articles, and camera. Canoe, paddles, camp equipment, and food are furnished at a rate of approximately six dollars a day per individual patron. Guides can be hired at an additional cost of from twelve to fifteen dollars per day. Reservations should be made in advance.

Outfitters usually are established at or near embarkation points. In selecting an outfitter, it is well to learn from him whether the route leading from his base of operations is traveled heavily; whether there are alternative, wilder routes away from normal travel; the general nature of the water and country on these routes; the kind of canoes and camp equipment he supplies; the list of foods he offers in his prescribed budget; and other particulars of special interest to the party. Highly illustrated folders with price lists are available, and the backs of such folders, generally, are maps of the region. It is possible to rent just a canoe or other parts of general equipment. When making inquiries for possible reservation, the outfitter likes to know:

1. The date that you plan to arrive, and the number of days that you expect to be on your trip.
2. The number in your party and their sex.
3. Equipment wanted. If complete outfitting, state the number of tents desired. If partial outfitting, list the items needed.

4. The type of trips you have in mind, and any special subjects of interest.
5. Your expected arrival time, and, if overnight, the accommodations desired.
6. If you are interested in guide service.

A deposit of not less than five dollars per individual is usually required to assure the reservation.

Personal items that outfitters do not furnish on their regular schedule, and that you should take along, are: rain gear, clothing, fishing tackle, camera, knife, compass, flashlight, toilet articles, soap, sunglasses, and personal towels. (See Chapters 3 and 13 for particulars pertaining to these items. If one or more of these personal items are also required, special indication should be made in your reservations.)

While canoe outfitting is a well-established, highly organized business, many regions in remote areas do not always have the kind of outfitting that serves your purpose best. Equipment is apt to be heavy and bulky, such as canvas tents instead of the light, sailcloth type. Canoes may be the close-ribbed, heavy-freighting type when standard paddling canoes are desired. It is wise, therefore, to get all particulars of equipment before actually making the reservation. If a satisfactory outfitter does not happen to be located where you wish to embark, arrange to have the right kind of equipment bonded and shipped to the embarkation point of your choice.

Generally, well-advertised canoe outfitters maintain their equipment at a satisfactory level. There is a heavy depreciation of equipment through camper inexperience. While repair and adjustment of equipment are a continuous process, most often well maintained, it is, nevertheless, best to examine tents for good repair, and see that they have adequate pitching ropes. If the water route requires it, be sure that you have tracking lines as suggested in Chapter 4. You must have an extra paddle and individual life preservers to comply with Canadian regulations. Be sure that you have canoe mending materials; and don't forget your fishing license.

A list of canoe outfitters can be found in the advertisements that appear in sporting magazines, generally in the issues at the close of winter, and just before the canoe season opens.

While canoe outfitters have a standard list of provisions which they supply, it is a good idea to obtain a list of these foods from them in advance for your own taste modification. Another plan is to suggest to the outfitter that you make the selection from his stock when you arrive, if you are a fussy eater. Some outfitters place strong emphasis on dehydrated foods. There is no objection to this, but if the trip is not of long duration, it is well to cut back on too many meals of the dehydrated kind, and carry some staple items. (For a treatment of this subject, see Informational Appendix.)

Those who have little or no experience in canoe travel, and wish to avoid the cost of a guide, can acquire a valuable initial start by having a guide spend only the first day with them on some island or point removed a short distance from the outfitter. He can show tent pitching methods, setting up a cooking fire and preparing a meal, devote a few hours to the proper handling of the canoe, and generally fill in his party on a practical approach to the trip. Some outfitters provide this kind of preliminary instruction as an integral part of their program.

General Notes for the Outfitter

Correspondence by the outfitter with prospective canoe patrons can become an arduous task if letters have to be answered at great length. Some make the error of simply inserting folders that answer the current questions in print. Most questions can best be answered more fully by this method, or by mimeo, but a letter should always accompany such material to assure the friendly relationship that a patron needs on entering a wilderness area. Where a man and a woman are associated with the outfitting, it is also wise to give the intimacy of first names on stationery and folders, such as Alice and Dale Doe. Many women accompany men on canoe trips, and the feminine member of the management provides women patrons with confidence in a strange country of largely male activity.

By a trial-and-error, experimental plan, advertising can be placed at a time of year that will build up the clientele for the coming season rather early. But if the ads are run too early, the moods for next season's canoe trip may not be built up in the minds of prospective canoeists. A good advertising time method to follow is to observe the number of canoe outfitting ads that appear in sporting magazines at a particular month of the year. However, the larger outfitters are generally willing to risk some advertising at all times of the year, even though it does not pay off to the same degree that a more opportune advertising period does. The new outfitter has to watch his budget more carefully, and should follow the trend of the top season advertising period until he gains patronage.

There is nothing that downgrades a canoe outfitter

more quickly than to supply equipment in poor repair, or equipment so badly depreciated that it gives risky service, especially in bad weather. Canoeists are encouraged when they enter upon their voyages with substantial new-looking equipment. Remember that they have entered upon an experience about which they will do a lot of talking, and that this is valuable advertising if it is praise for the outfitter and his equipment. The outfitter, therefore, should not only keep his equipment in the best repair, but should replace it whenever he feels that his original investment has been reasonably justified. He should bear in mind that most of his equipment is purchased on a wholesale basis, and that if he will sell off equipment to private individuals before it is too far depreciated, he can recover much of his wholesale cost. This is especially true of canoes, which have a rather high resale value. The important thing is to sell these items when they are still in good usable condition. Thus the outfitter can replace his stock regularly, and advertise that it is well maintained.

Canoes suffer considerable depreciation at the hands of inexperienced canoeists. Aluminum canoes can be supplied with auxiliary bang plates attached to the bows of canoes by a welder. The cost of the bang plates is small compared to the great saving in canoe depreciation.

Tents should be well reinforced at the points where ropes are attached, and in the waterproofing process there should be a small quantity of clear creosote, or other preservative, added to preserve the tents from early rot. You should never issue a tent that looks as if it may deteriorate on the trail. If the canoeist suffers from prolonged exposure by reason of a rotten tent in bad weather, the outfitter may be subject to a damage suit. Tents should be of the type that are a combination of high convertibility and easy pitching. (See "Convertible Wedge Tent" in my book, *The New Way of the Wilderness*, published by The Macmillan Company.) If the outfitter will have a printed fabric swatch attached to the tent, showing a simple pitching principle (see Chapter 13, page 180), the depreciation will be less, and the canoeist will be grateful for the information. Allow generous rope lengths. Short ropes contribute to tent depreciation through bad pitching. Ropes also should be treated, as described above, to prevent rot.

Packsacks suffer severe depreciation. A strap torn loose from a pack can become a great inconvenience out on the trail, and is a tough one on which to give an emergency mend. Pack straps of leather usually outlast the canvas part. If the outfitter has a shoemaker's sewing machine, he can replace canvas portions. If he completely removes the depreciated canvas portions and the rivets himself, and sends the straps in for attaching to new canvas, this becomes economically practical. If the outfitter will place another printed fabric swatch on all packsacks, showing how to pick up a packsack by the "ears" (see *The New Way of the Wilderness*), he will save much depreciation, and the canoeist will take some pride in knowing the best handling of this item.

We have gradually been entering upon an era when canoes in many instances have to be supplied with outboard motors. (A broad treatment of this subject is given in Chapter 4.) The outfitter should give careful consideration to motor weight. In an upset, a heavy motor can drown the canoeists, for it will set the canoe on end in the water, offering little chance to use the canoe for life-preserving buoyancy.

The outfitter itemizes all equipment issued to the patron, and has him sign the list. Sometimes these lists carry frightening commitments for the canoeist where he agrees to pay for lost equipment, depreciation, and takes other responsibilities. The question arises whether these demands upon the patron should be made. They savor too much of distrust. I think they should be deleted entirely, the patron only signing out his equipment. If there is some loss, the canoeist is generally willing to pay for it without his being committed to a written agreement. Extravagant losses are few, and perhaps the outfitter will gain more in the final analysis simply by marking it down to current expense.

Lastly, consider that there will always be a continuous depreciation and loss of equipment from inexperienced users, and that if you incur ulcer reactions to these daily misfortunes, you should not be in the canoe outfitting business. Regard your losses and depreciation not as individual strokes of misfortune but on an aggregate basis, and balance them against your profits. I think that a generous and tolerant attitude toward patrons will pay off, not only as a business asset, but in health and general well-being for the outfitter.

Some campers prefer cooking on gasoline or propane stoves. These should be kept on hand for such patrons and for the times when the Forestry Service forbids campfires because of a hazardous humidity level. Attach clear instructions for operating these stoves, and what to do when they become fouled up.

Is the canoeist able to handle the dehydrated foods or does he prefer the more staple kinds of food? Many campers get a certain wilderness romance out of the dehydrated foods, and will insist upon them, but it is wise to lay emphasis on the optional choice of foods.

12 PROFESSIONAL AND COMMERCIAL CANOE TRAVEL

EARLIER, I indicated that exploration for the purpose of discovering unknown areas had given way to reexploration by scientific studies of remote wilderness regions. These scientific ventures have become just as attractive to inquiring and professional minds as were the early historic expeditions into unknown lands. The great importance of initially discovering these lands should in no way subordinate the comparable importance of rediscovery for scientific or even lay purposes.

Every morning when the rumble of traffic in urban centers signals another day of industry, a significant number of men step into their canoes in the wilderness, embarking on various government projects of reexploration: geodetic surveys, geophysics, forestry, and a host of other interests of national welfare. No less is the amount of private activity: prospecting, commercial fisheries, mining, and others.

It would be misleading here to stress only the strictly professional or scientific results. A vast amount of valuable knowledge is contributed by small, nonprofessional research canoe parties, for semiprofessional ends, and this information is ultimately classified as professionally documented material.

Small groups from educational institutions studying, perhaps, the nesting habits of birds; students of geology doing fieldwork during vacations, or students doing a study of races for a major in ethnology; and numerous other inquiring groups and individuals are among those who embark upon canoe journeys.

Geotechnological parties entering wilderness areas to check on mining claims, survey groups establishing base and meridian lines far in the interior, and other such operations where a considerable number of men are required in a party generally call for semipermanent camps, or camps made permanent over the period of the operation. This entails moving large amounts of equipment, but not necessarily large canoes.

The procedure in the North today, where the operations are to take place in an area of lakes, rivers, and creeks, is to fly in the equipment and provisions, including small canoes, by water-based planes or, in certain restricted land areas, by helicopter. Where the work is to be done on large lakes, requiring freighting canoes, movement of these canoes is generally made by canoeists to the point of the operations, where, of course, a canoe route is available to the operation site. (If the operation is a very large one, where cost of flying in the equipment is excessive, consideration should be given to moving in all the equipment, including canoes, the previous winter by caterpillar train, over the lake ice and intermediate land-cut trails.)

When speed is important in moving freighting canoes to the operation, the crew generally travels with only a very light camp outfit and with just enough provisions to complete the trip. It has been found, however, that the cost of flying in freight is not always a saving in labor cost. It depends on the kind of canoe water, in relation to the portages, that the freighting job entails. The Hudson's Bay Company has often employed Indians for transporting store supplies over long water routes by canoe, instead of flying in the loads where the cost was the same, because it gave employment to Indians during a season when they could not occupy themselves with trapping or other remunerative effort.

In remote places where a supply ship touches port only once each year, a canoe route from the port nearest the operations may greatly reduce the transportation task. Under such circumstances, it may be necessary to ship the large freighting canoes and equipment to this port the previous season for storage through the winter. Hudson Bay posts can be good commercial storage points in such instances.

Expeditions that employ large groups of men have difficulty in operating on the same diet as the small parties traveling by canoe not serviced by a plane. Dehydrated foods, which form part of the average canoe trip fare, are generally looked upon with disdain by men who spend long periods at hard labor in the wilderness. There is a human relationship problem, too, which leaders of expeditions must consider. If the expedition is to remain in the wilderness for a long period, it should be serviced by a smaller plane, at scheduled intervals, carrying fresh foods and such luxury items as will excite the appetites and raise the spirits of the crew. A demand for luxury foods seems to have increased among moderns doing manual labor in the wilderness. The point is, of course, that old privations are now unnecessary with the advent of plane transportation—a fact made too apparent, perhaps, to a crew of men whose interest is chiefly employment and physical comfort. This has been most evident where crews have been flown in from outlying settlements to fight fires.

Another important advantage in periodic flights with fresh foods is that the men can also get mail at more frequent intervals, which is good for morale.

In commercial endeavors, consider carefully whether canoes need outboard motors, or whether the distance from the semipermanent camp to local operations can readily be paddled. The cost and inconvenience of flying in needless outboard motor fuel can raise the bills of an expedition and complicate operations, especially on the tundra, where commercial fuel is also used for cooking and heating.

Sheet metal camp stoves, with ovens using wood for fuel in forested areas, are the standard cooking units in permanent camps. On the arctic prairie, where commercial fuel is essential for cooking, the pressure cooker and thermos jugs will save considerable fuel. Baked beans, bean soup, pea soup, and other items that require long cooking can either be cooked in the pressure cooker, or brought to maximum heat in a cooking pail and then quickly transferred to the thermos jugs. If the jugs are also covered with wool garments or a blanket, the food will, to a certain degree, continue to cook for most of the night, as in the old fireless cooker.

After completion of a commercial operation in a remote region, it may be unwise to transport the heavy equipment, such as wall tents and stoves, to the outside. Depreciation can be severe enough to warrant leaving this equipment in the wilderness. I have come upon such abandoned camps from time to time. Indians in the region may occupy these camps as they pass through, but they seem to have a strong sense of equity in ownership, and will not remove equipment without permission. Such permission ought to be forwarded to the Indians whenever equipment is permanently abandoned.

Prospectors, geotechnological staffs, and others who set up semipermanent and permanent camps should keep their canoes as much within the range of practical portage weight as possible. Heavy canoes have a way of frustrating efforts to search for minerals or for carrying on activity into offbeat places.

Where forest fires rage far from a body of water, booster pumps are needed at properly spaced intervals along the hose line. The spacing of such booster pumps depends on steepness of terrain. Along with the use of folding canvas tanks at these booster points, from which the water is repumped, canoes are often put into service as tanks, the light aluminum canoes being excellent for this purpose, paddled and portaged to these points, or sent in by helicopter.

Fire fighting can be a dirty job, but crews are not at a loss to supply a solution. I saw three aluminum canoes in service as bathtubs, one being used directly over a fire to heat water. While the water level was maintained in the canoe, there seemed to be no apparent damage from the open fire; but I emphatically do not recommend the canoe as a water heater. As a bathtub, yes—perhaps.

13 CANOE VOYAGE EQUIPMENT AND ITS USE

THE human being is the only creature who fares badly in the wilderness without tools. Yet, if he overburdens himself with equipment, he impedes his freedom of travel.

Against these two opposing premises, the canoe voyager must consider what he needs to sustain himself. The difficulty will be to arrive at a point of compromise between too much equipment and too little. Generally, he hauls along too much—gadgets intended to make life easy, but which turn out to be a nuisance around camp, a handicap and burden over every portage trail.

But, all too frequently, piddling novelties are passed off for "go-light" equipment, which seriously impair practical living and create needless physical and mental stress. The victims of novelties are not, as a rule, made aware that the gradual disinterest they develop on a single wilderness jorney may be attributed to impractical equipment. They come to accept the discomforts of badly applied items as inevitable. This, I think, accounts for the large number who enter the wilderness each season, and resolve at the end of their ordeal never to go again. Many never do. A happy share manage to see through the fog of their miscalculations, and discover that life in the wilderness can be a rich and pleasant experience if proper equipment, provisions, and proved methods are employed.

Centuries of canoe-travel experience have screened out most impractical ideas, and retained some fairly sound principles in equipment, provisions, and methods, which should be recognized and given careful consideration before being replaced by pet innovations, or scanty versions of practical equipment.

Next to the tendency toward contraction of equipment to the point of impairment, misapplication of equipment runs a close second. For example, the pack frame and the mountain climber's pack creep into canoe-travel equipment where these items have no practical place. The advocates of these packs will give you the most logical reason why pack frames, instead of the standard Duluth packsack, should be used on canoe trips. If the advocate stays with canoe travel long enough to test his misapplication, the pack frame quietly disappears from his canoe equipment.

Canoe travel requires a wholly different kind of equipment from that used on pack trips. Portage trails do call for a share of back packing, but this does not alter the main issue. If, for example, we take an average of portage trails and water, we find that the route from the mouth of the St. Lawrence River to the mouth of the Yukon River calls for approximately seven thousand miles of water and a hundred and fifty miles of portage trails, or roughly one mile of portage to every fifty miles of water. This proportion will vary from route to route, of course, but there can be no justification for applying mountain pack-frame methods, poorly adapted to canoe travel, where most of the travel is by water, or using mountain climbing footwear where in an upset such footwear would make drowning almost certain.

Emphasis on "going light" has so dominated canoe travel that the advice becomes dogmatic and misleading. Tents get meager and doghousy, and a week of steady rain makes camp life a form of imprisonment. Camp axes are so puny they couldn't possibly be used to cut out portage trails or cut through down timber across an obstructed wilderness stream. Canoes can be so small that they sag to dangerous freeboard levels, and become dulling drags with paddles, often keeping the occupants windbound in any heavy-running sea.

Going light for mobility's sake is, of course, sound in principle if utility does not suffer. The equation of utility and mobility is not easily calculated. But, we can suggest that spending a half-hour or more each day building a bough bed rather than carrying along a 1½ pound air mattress is a needless exertion at the end of a hard day of travel. If we insist that the fragrance of balsam boughs is worth the labor of a bough bed—a poor substitute for an air mattress—one or two boughs under the pillow for fragrance will do the trick. If we have to hack away for an hour with a tiny hatchet—or, more likely, not be able to cut through down timber across an obstructed stream —rather than carry a three-quarter cruising ax, which would accomplish the job with a minimum of labor, we are, of course, deluded.

A marked change is taking place among prospectors and explorer groups who travel deep in wilderness areas for long periods. Because of the lightness of aluminum canoes and the closely woven, light tent materials, both canoes and tents are gradually becoming larger and more adaptable. With the advent of canoe outboard motors, which use gasoline, primus gasoline stoves and gasoline lanterns are now commonly being included.

For the go-light canoe-tripper, with an addiction to scanty tents and small canoes, these may, of course, seem a perversion. Much of the move to more practical equipment is the result of commercial and pleasure trips being flown into remote areas—the actual canoe travel then being confined to the local areas. But this more practical-sized equipment is also coming into use on the long canoe trip where extensive utilitarian living becomes essential.

The dogmatic go-lighter is not usually the inveterate traveler who spends long periods or full seasons of varying weather in the wilderness, but he is an admirable fellow. He does much planning, and makes fairly substantial wilderness trips—generally the full extent of his vacation—during carefully selected seasonal periods. When he returns, you will have a convincing story from him of go-light camping gear. He has the earmarks of an expert, at least to the uninitiated.

But if, for some reason, his program changes, and he must spend long periods of seasonal overlap in the wilderness professionally, he gradually becomes disillusioned. He discovers that days on end of rain, extreme temperature changes in the transition of seasons, insects, and a hundred other encumbering and frustrating factors of protracted wilderness living might be overcome by the simple addition of a pair of pocket-size gasoline cooking units, a roomier, more livable tent, a larger canoe for rapids and rough seas, and otherwise more practical gear. The actual difference in portage weight is negligible. Performing essential camp tasks and having diversion away from bugs; out of the rain; sheltered from a raw, cold, and devastating wind, he begins to feel an adjustment to wilderness life, a sense of well-being and an all-season mastery over the elements that is very reassuring. For a while he suffers a certain guilt because he cannot equate his new and practical advantages with his dogmatic, miniaturized go-lightness. Gradually, he adjusts to the more utilitarian equipment, and realizes that his amateur days are over. He becomes a more mature woodsman.

The risk of suggesting practical equipment over go-light gear is that the uninitiated are apt to take this as license to bring along all manner of cumbersome, heavy equipment—even worse in its consequences than the piddling variety.

The problem presents a need for realism. If we go entirely by paddle, and speed is not important, we may perhaps be closer to the elemental wilderness than if we included the outboard motor and a supply of gasoline. Where we go by paddle, we travel a great deal more slowly on the water, and, surprisingly enough, only a little faster on the portages. The added load of motor, gas, a seaworthy canoe, and a roomier tent has to be figured on the ratio of a great many miles of water—much of it against fast currents and head winds—to each mile of portage. Thus, the party with a heavier load and outboard motor will progress faster than the go-light party using paddles—in most North American canoe country. This would not apply where a long series of cascades makes it necessary to portage more frequently, but we must consider averages on extensive travel. Short trips generally entail no problem.

Speed may be important to the prospector, or it may be

important to the individual pleasure-tripper, who wants
to reach remote regions, and benefit most by them in the
time allotted to him. The argument that a motor incurs
more work on portages than it is worth on the water is
not valid. The fruitless labor of fighting head-on seas or
many miles of extremely fast water with a paddle or by
tracking overbalances the extra labor on the portages.

Much of this, of course, resolves itself into what each
considers the greatest values for him on a canoe trip. On
pleasure trips, we need to seek the peace and contentment
of the wilderness—not speed. And I would most certainly
recommend, where practical, going by paddle and with a
go-light outfit of sensible selection, in preference to travel
by motor. Rationality and artful approach—even our
deepest sentiments—must, of course, prevail, certainly not
dogma. On a trip of several months, hundreds of miles
may be, and should be, for peaceful and intelligent diversion, the course propelled by paddle, the outboard motor
lying dormant in its canvas cover whenever feasible;
sometimes a "squaw" sail may be used with a favorable
wind; but there are times when the outboard motor needs
to go into its working position for long hours of forcing
one's way up through a mountain river as fast as a mill-
race, or coursing many obstinate miles through a heavy-
running sea, where paddling would prove futile or result
in keeping the canoeist windbound.

The important thing is to apply whatever facilities are
needed, whether they be for cold practicability, capricious and romantic mood, or fortuitous circumstance.
Where a motorized canoe usurps the desired quiet solitude
of canoe and paddle, we lose. When we forego the use of
the motor in order to maintain some traditional sentimen-
tality about the paddle, in water that allows little or no

progress with paddles, we also lose. It is possible to combine both if we use a mature sense of discrimination.

A book on wilderness canoe country can, after all, only suggest certain equipment and methods—possibly values —but should never impose a choice or outlook. The final decision, whatever the event, is always the reader's.

Toward the end of this chapter, some items that require special description are treated in detail. Those not requiring such description are simply listed in the Informational Appendix.

TENTS

Any tent that cannot readily be converted in a matter of minutes to provide protection under varying conditions of heat, cold, rain, snow, changing wind, and insects, ought to be rejected. Nonconvertible cloth cells, of which there are a great variety of styles and designs—but which are not essentially different in principle—come under this heading. (Exceptions are large wall tents for semipermanent camps; and the lightweight, double-wall, arctic, pyramid tent, used only in arctic winter travel; but neither of these is adaptable for the canoe voyage.)

Weather conditions confronting the canoe voyager over the North American continent are extremely variable. In the North, he may start his voyage immediately after the spring breakup, when temperatures vary from freezing at night to 60 degrees during the day. This range of temperature may, of course, continue to rise as spring progresses. But weather can suddenly change adversely, and cold weather is often projected unseasonably into late spring, or it appears prematurely in the fall.

About ten years ago I entered Canada on a voyage well

after spring breakup time, when the noon temperature stood at 70 degrees. Within a week, I encountered a snowfall that dropped 18 inches of snow in four days. Farther south, we have conditions of excessive heat and rain; but we should not think that heat is not also a problem in the Far North. The temperature has been known, on occasion, to reach close to 100 degrees within the Arctic Circle during the season of the midnight sun, when the earth is heated through a big part of each 24 hours.

A rough list of requirements in tent design, therefore, runs about as follows:

Simple to pitch for rapid encampment.

Adaptable as a lean-to for reflecting an open fire in cold weather.

Adaptable as a canopy-shelter to maintain a drying fire during rain, under which to cook, eat, and perform camp tasks. This drying feature is needed primarily to reduce moisture in sleeping gear and clothing caused by high humidity.

Easily convertible for sudden shifts of blowing rain, or ability to be closed entirely to allow sheer drainage sides in a heavy downpour.

Readily opened from any side to allow free view over the water area and general landscape for diversion during prolonged rains without wetting the occupants.

Full area cross-ventilation to allow maximum movement of air during hot periods.

Light in weight, of very high-count material, but large enough for free living. About 7′ × 9′ for two people.

Amply protected from insects. Insect netting sewn to tent openings is not wholly satisfactory. A netting

A Re-Design from the Basic Wedge of a Tent. Insert Shows Convertible Feature

the size and shape of the tent should be hung from loops sewn on the inside of the tent ridge. Tie-tapes on the netting provide the fastening. Such netting will permit removing the mosquito tent entirely for protection from insects away from the tent, at points where meals—especially at noontime—will be served, or in blinds where observations of wildlife and photography may be done. Quickly suspended between trees, the four corners can be brought out and temporarily held down with small stones or sticks. A strip of cloth sewn around the lower edge of the netting gives it a better draping weight. Mosquito netting preferably should be dyed a dark, neutral color to permit better vision through the mesh. White netting reflects light, blurring the vision.

Equipped with a sod cloth and removable ground sheet, the ground sheet to be used for tumpline packing and as a tarpaulin. (The sod cloth is a strip of material sewn to the bottom of the tent, turned inside as a ground seal.) Over this sod cloth goes the ground sheet. Where the same tent is to be used for winter travel, this sod cloth is turned outside the tent. (For winter camping and wilderness travel, see my book, *The New Way of the Wilderness*, The Macmillan Company.)

The accompanying tent illustrations show the different methods of pitching the tent and adapting it to various weather conditions. The tent illustrated is a redesign of the basic wedge tent. Tent openings have been split at both ends to the ridge, so that either half of the tent can be raised as a canopy, or both raised to form one large canopy. (The name and address of tentmakers authorized to manufacture this tent will be furnished by me upon request addressed in care of the publisher.)

Tents must be accurately pitched each time to their intended shape, or they will lose their essential, smooth, unwrinkled, rain-shedding surfaces. Wedge tents are rectangular or square at the base, and may be pitched as follows: Stake and tie down the two bottom rear corners of the tent. Take hold of the two bottom front corners, bring them together, and draw them out taut to form a triangle on the ground. The point of the triangle is the exact center line of your tent from front to back. Now bring out each front corner which you are holding from this center line to each side, exactly half the width of your tent from the center line, and stake down these front corners. You will then have a perfect rectangle. Use taut-line hitches for tying the ridge to trees or stakes—for easy adjustment without untying the knot. Use clove hitches on the ridge rope around the tent pole. The height of the knot along the pole can then be adjusted, and the position of the poles moved toward or away from the tent without untying the clove hitch. Use bowline knots for attaching ropes to tent loops, for ease in untying, when using the ropes for other purposes. (See illustrations of these knots.)

Light cotton tent materials of exceptionally high thread count, waterproofed at the factory with copper compounds, are the most successful. Always dry tents thoroughly before storing. This is best done while the tent has a perfect pitch on a level spot. It will then assume its proper shape for folding.

CANOE AND PADDLES

For most average canoe travel, the 18-foot lightweight aluminum; the 18-foot American canvas; and the 17-foot Canadian wood-and-canvas canoes—all in either Prospec-

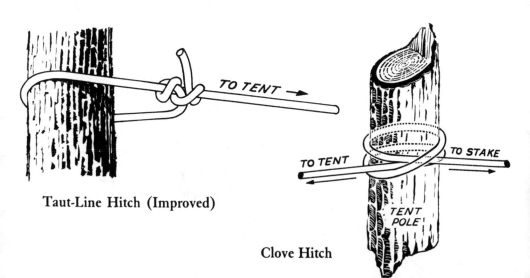

Taut-Line Hitch (Improved)

Clove Hitch

tor or Guide's models—will serve; also, where Fiberglas
canoes are available, the Guide's or Prospector models.
(See Chapter 2.) For the rougher mountain rivers, where
there are extremely heavy rapids, or on the Great Lakes
and other large waters, such as Great Bear and Great
Slave lakes, the 20-foot aluminum, or the 18-, 20-, or
22-foot canvas canoe should be selected. The 19-foot,
square stern, aluminum canoe is the same as the 20-foot
paddling type, except that the stern has been cut short 1
foot for application of the square transom. Small canoes
can, of course, be used on large water, but layovers should
be made when seas are running heavily.

Most rugged paddles are made of white ash, and these
are preferred. Ash wood varies greatly in weight, so select
light ones. If a good quality of white spruce is available,
this makes a light paddle—sometimes preferred to the
heavier ash. Maple makes a good paddle, but is heavy.
Choose the length of paddle that suits you. As described
earlier, when resting vertically on the ground, the paddle
should reach to somewhere between your eyes and your
chin. Be sure that the edges of the blade are thin enough
to feather well (cut the water) without a noisy ripple. If

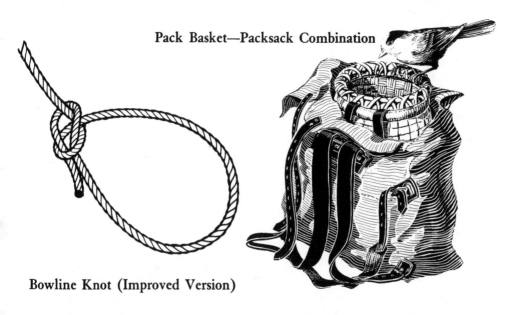

Pack Basket—Packsack Combination

Bowline Knot (Improved Version)

they are not thin, plane or rasp down the edges to about one-eighth inch.

PACKING EQUIPMENT

Duluth packsacks with leather shoulder and head straps, in the No. 2 size, 26″×28″ and the No. 3 size, 28″× 30″ are the traditional, proved canoe packsacks used for clothing, general equipment, and all foods that are contained in bags, such as cereals, sugar, et cetera. A packsack should first be lined with a waterproof bag. Army surplus stores have clothesbags large enough to fit into these packsacks. If these are not available, liners can be custom made or homemade from thin, waterproof, airtight, rubberized material and shoemaker's latex cement. This will keep equipment and provisions from getting wet in rains or upsets.

All hard items that might gouge your back should be carried in the large 22″ pack basket. These include such canned items as jam, peanut butter, et cetera. If you value your peace of mind on long trips, do not carry these items in plastic envelopes. You cannot imagine the mess that results from breakage.

Pack baskets come supplied with a pack harness and a canvas cover—a bad combination. The pack carries awkwardly and is poorly protected from rain or upset. Discard the harness and canvas cover and, instead, slip a thin, waterproof bag into the pack basket, then insert this combination into a packsack. The waterproof liner bag is first tied shut, and then the flap on the packsack is strapped down over that. Now, you have a pack that will not gouge you, will carry well with the shoulder straps and head strap of the packsack, and will float indefinitely in an upset. Woven, basketlike clothes hampers, with lids removed, may be used in the same manner as pack baskets.

Never carry tent, sleeping bags, or air mattresses in packsacks or duffel bags. It is exasperating to stuff these bulky items into, and pull them out of, tight packs at every camp. The following method allows expedient packing of these items, and greatly facilitates encamping and decamping:

Lay out the waterproof ground sheet from your tent—full length and width. On the lengthwise center one-third of the ground sheet, lay your air mattresses, leaving one foot at the end of the ground sheet exposed for a waterproof seal. On the air mattresses, lay your tent, if it is dry. (If it is not dry, pack it on the outside.) On the tent, lay your sleeping bags. Now fold the right and the left one-third of your ground sheet over the various items. Start rolling the pack from the opposite end from where you left the 1-foot seal mentioned above, and continue to roll these items into a tight pack. Tie the whole pack with a piece of No. 5 sash cord to keep it from unrolling. Then lash the roll with either the tumpline or the pack harness as shown in the accompanying illustrations. This packing method quickly disposes of all your bulky items in one operation.

TUMPLINE

A tumpline simply consists of two 8-foot latigo leather straps sewn to a wider leather head strap. The head strap should fit on top and forward of the head, just above the forehead—not *on* the forehead. You will feel the proper position of the head strap when your load is carried with the most comfortable center of gravity. While walking, one or both hands should support the tumplines at a position near the neck, to prevent a forward or backward tug of the head. (See the illustration.) Once you have learned to pack with a tumpline, you may like it better than the shoulder straps. The early fur trade packers traditionally used this method. The advantage is in not having straps dig into the soft tissues of the shoulders. This strap discomfort is not felt on the head.

PACK HARNESS

Some people find difficulty in using the tumpline. Generally, this is because of improper use or weak neck muscles. If you come to the conclusion, after a valiant effort, that you cannot pack with a tumpline, make a pack harness, or have it made by a harnessmaker or shoemaker. The illustration gives full details for making such a harness. As you can see, it is equipped with shoulder and head straps. Tent and bedroll, duffel bag, a sack of flour, or any other pack may be strapped into the harness and then carried with the shoulder straps, or both shoulder and head straps, in the same manner as a Duluth packsack.

PROTECTIVE CONTAINERS

Items that require protection can be carried in a rather ingenious improvisation made by inserting a gallon-size oil or antifreeze can into a drawstring bag. The Army surplus ditty bag is the right size—or a bag can easily be made. This is a crushproof container well suited to carry many easily crushed, small items.

Tumpline Packing

Pack Harness

AX WITH SHEATH

For most canoe travel, the ax should be a single-bit, three-quarter cruiser size, with a curved hickory handle— the blade ground to a fairly thin edge for chopping, and the ax kept well sheathed when not in use. The sheath is best made of two pieces of leather, with two pieces of thin, spring brass sandwiched in between, and the four pieces riveted together with copper rivets. (See illustration.) Two thongs tie the sheath to the ax head.

KNIFE WITH SHEATH

You can get along very well with a jackknife; but if you need to make a paddle, a sheath knife makes a better draw knife, and the filleting of fish needs more length than the jackknife blade. Select a sheath knife with a fairly thin blade. The thick, chisel-like, pig-sticking type of knife so abundant on the market is only a handicap tool. Avoid stainless steel knives; they are too soft to hold an edge. Sheaths that come with most knives are poor and hazardous. Make your own leather knife sheath, or have it made, and line it with thin sheet brass for safety. A small penknife is often useful.

WHETSTONES AND FILE

A flat mill file is needed to keep the ax in shape, if the edge gets rough treatment. Canadian firms make a standard ax file. Generally, this sharpening job, when not too rough, can be handled with a stone. A double-faced, fine and coarse India stone is the best available for putting on

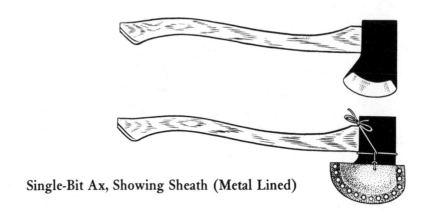

Single-Bit Ax, Showing Sheath (Metal Lined)

Belt Knife Sheath (Metal Lined)

Set of "Billies" with Bowl Lids

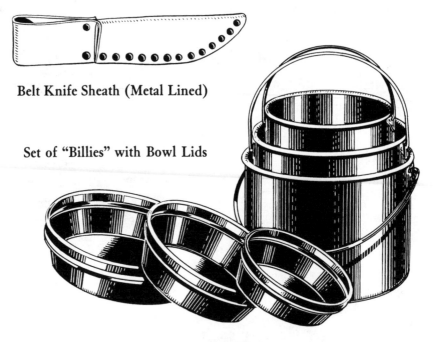

Original Copper Tea Pail
of the Early Fur Trade—
Now Priceless Artifact

a good edge. This should be about four inches long. For fine finishing of the ax edge, for whetting knives, and for sharpening fishhooks, a small, soft Arkansas slipstone is excellent. Both of these stones can be ordered by your hardware dealer. Because they are more expensive than the black gritstones, they are generally not stocked.

COOKING KIT

Aluminum pails or "billies" that nest and are equipped with wire bails for hanging them over a fire are the most suitable utensils for cooking in the wilderness. Tinned nesting pails should be avoided. The tinned coating melts off with the heat of repeated fires, and the pails rust. One type of aluminum nesting pail comes with inverted serving bowls fitted as covers—a valuable, compact, and go-light feature. (See illustration.) Aluminum cups are rapid heat conductors and too hot for the lips. Stainless steel cups, available from outfitters, are quite satisfactory. Stainless steel, or black steel frying pans with detachable long handles, should be used instead of the aluminum ones that come with the nested sets. Food sticks to most aluminum frypans. Folding reflector ovens do the baking job, and will bake everything from biscuits and apple cobblers to fish and meat. The baking of bread can also be done with a frying pan, bannock fashion. (See illustration both of reflector oven and bannock pan-baking methods on pp. 213 and 215.)

FOOD CONTAINERS

All dry foods should be placed in thin, polyethylene bags, these in turn placed in cloth bags with tie-strings for secure closing. The tie-strings must be sewn to the bags at the center to prevent losing them. Jam, butter, and similar items go into friction-top, press-on, tinned cans. Do not carry food items in the original, fragile, store containers, such as cardboard and plastic. Before packing such items, transfer them to the bag or tin containers which I have mentioned. Semisoft plastic containers with screw-top lids are sold for carrying such items as jam and other soft foods, but the materials of these containers, I have found, absorb and hold food odors, setting up putrefaction. Hard plastic containers crack in time—apparently from chemical and physical change. For safety, use metal, friction-top containers. Metal containers should be coated inside, for food protection, with pure beeswax, by heating the wax and pouring it in and out of the can. Carry these canned items in the pack-basket-packsack combination described.

LIGHTING UNITS

The folding aluminum candle lantern was the old illumination standby on wilderness trips for centuries. Artificial light was considered a luxury, and was usually eliminated. The lone candle was sometimes propped up in a tent—often held in a split stick sharpened and stuck into the ground—but it was a fire hazard. The flashlight has held its own as a camp light in late years. The Boy Scout flashlight with the right-angle head is the most convenient type because it can be hung in the tent at a good angle for illumination by its clip. The evening campfire usually provides ample light in the camp area for most movement.

The carbide light has been in use for many years, and is about the brightest light for its weight and size. The jet orifice must be kept open by periodically probing it with a very fine wire filament (furnished with the light), each time it is used, or it gets plugged, and nothing else fine enough for this cleaning can be improvised on the trail. A packet of these wires should be carried as spares. Always blow out carbide lamps before shutting them off. When the flame is allowed to die after being shut off, a carbon deposit forms, and plugs the orifice. The open flame of a carbide lamp, like a candle, is also a fire hazard to be watched.

The gasoline lantern gives an excellent light, equivalent to about a hundred-watt electric bulb—but the lantern is bulky. The mantles are fragile, but they stand a surprising amount of jarring. Unburned mantles that are unbreakable until burned off are carried for spares. The gasoline lantern provides considerable heat in a tent, and, of course, makes reading a regular luxury. Propane mantle lanterns are convenient, but they are usually bulky, and are too uneconomical of fuel to be practical on canoe trips of any great length.

Never walk off into wooded or brushy areas at night without a flashlight. Serious eye injuries can be caused this way.

GASOLINE AND OTHER STOVES

Throughout the arctic tundra, the Swedish primus stove has been used for a great many years. It operates on kerosene, and is primed with alcohol. Many variations of this stove for cooking and for heating a tent have been developed over the years, so that now we have pocket-size both gasoline and kerosene stoves, in the primus and other makes, that add very little weight to the canoe outfit.

Two of these pocket-size stoves will cook a substantial meal in about the same time required on the burners of a home range. Most of the stoves weigh approximately one and a half pounds and take up very little room in the pack. They add a great deal of comfort during wet, blowing weather, when outdoor cooking over an open fire is inconvenient. The common, two-burner, gasoline camp stove of the suitcase shape is a practical unit, but much too bulky and heavy for canoe travel. With a little ingenuity, a full meal can be cooked on just one of the small, pocket-size primus stoves.

The propane stove in this type, like the lantern, is bulky and too uneconomical of fuel for canoe trips.

While the above heating units are very compact, and serve most heating needs for a tent in canoe weather, the modern heating unit of the catalytic type should be used where greater capacity or all-night heating is required, since it is free from dangerous fumes without having to be vented.

Even small, sheet metal, wood-burning stoves have been used on canoe travel where the weather tends to be cold, rainy, and rough. Since these stoves have to be sheet metal, the box or "Yukon stove" made square, warps badly with intense heat. The best sheet metal stove is the smallest size—the so-called airtight unit—which weighs 6 pounds, has a top and bottom oval shape 12×16 inches, with a good flat top for cooking. Because of its rounded shape, it will stand excessive heat. It should be equipped with 4-inch pipe. Telescopic pipe, or separate, individual sections can be made up of a length that will store in the stove. For cleanliness, the stove should be carried in a canvas case, and, since it is not heavy, it can be tossed on top of a pack when carrying it over the portages. This, admittedly, is a bulky unit; but so light, it seems a small nuisance where cold, windy, rainy weather warrants its use. (For a full treatment of this unit for winter camping, which can also apply to canoe trips, see my book, *The New Way of the Wilderness*, The Macmillan Company.)

FIRST-AID KIT

It will pay you to make an office call to a physician who has had wilderness experience, and have him supply you with your needs, if you are going on a canoe journey extensive enough to warrant major first-aid consideration. He can, on prescription, supply items not otherwise available to you in a drugstore. Also, if he is one of the kind who has had a special interest in wilderness travel, he will be able to give you valuable firsthand instruction. Short of discussing first aid with your physician, you should, at least, carefully read a Red Cross First-Aid Manual before you set out on a major trip, and include such a manual with your outfit. First-Aid kits with simple items adaptable for the layman are, of course, sold in drugstores, or any druggist will pack a kit for you. The items should be placed in a waterproof, noncrush container. A metal or light wood box sealed with tape will do, or you can use a smaller version of the protective combination bag-and-can container described in this chapter. Carry the packed first-aid kit in the described pack-basket-packsack combination for best protection.

COMPASS

A pocket compass large enough to have a calibrated circle, from 1° to 360°, allows you to set your course more accurately than one with only cardinal and inter-cardinal points. (Chapter 5 contains a detailed treatment of this subject.)

MATCHES AND MATCH SAFE

Carry the main stock of matches in a sealed, water-proof, friction-top, metal can; the daily supply in a water-proof match safe—an item sold in all sporting goods stores. Buy the best large wooden stick matches for camp-fires. Do not depend wholly on lighters.

SLEEPING EQUIPMENT

Sleeping bag weight is a point of much discussion, but argument is pointless, because most canoe travel covers a wide range of temperatures, and one sleeping bag must serve for all. I have met this all-weather problem by a simple conversion method. Make or have made a down liner that is exactly square, so that for the conversion it can be folded crosswise or lengthwise of the down-filled tubes. When folded, it is put into a dyed sailcloth or similar high-count cotton material snap cover. Never

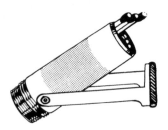

Waterproof Match Safe

use waterproof covers. Serious condensation would take place. During cold nights, the robe liner is folded lengthwise of the down-filled tubes, used with the down uniformly distributed through the liner. On warm nights when this maximum covering is excessive, I lay out the liner, roll it lengthwise with the tubes, and, in a matter of a minute or two, pat the down with the flat of my hand until much of it is moved along through the tubes to the other half of the liner. Now, when the down liner is unrolled and folded *across* instead of lengthwise of the tubes and then placed in the snap cover, most of the down is under the body—only enough left in the upper half to give proper cover for the particular night's warmer temperature. Variations of extreme temperatures can, thus, be met with only this single convertible unit by varying the amount of down over and under you. (For detailed instructions of how to construct this entire unit, see my book, *The New Way of the Wilderness*, published by The Macmillan Company.)

AIR MATTRESS

The air mattress can be full length or three-quarter, depending on the importance of the weight factor. Air mattresses are made in weights from 1½ pounds in short lengths to full length 32″×74″ size that are almost as thick and equally as soft as an innerspring mattress. Actually only that part of the body from the knees up requires cushioning. If you find that the air mattress is cold to lie on during early spring and late fall canoe travel, make incisions in the tubes, and insert a small amount of white goose down—not enough to prevent compact deflation of the mattress. While the incisions are open, a copper tube screen must be placed over the inside air vent to prevent feather clogging during deflation. The incisions can be resealed with inner-tube patching rubber and cement. The down will fluff up when the mattress is inflated and greatly improve the underbody warmth. Agitate the down after inflation to fluff and distribute it evenly through the mattress. Unless you want to court a nocturnal catastrophe, do not use plastic air mattresses.

OUTBOARD MOTORS

Outboard motors vary in size from 1 horsepower up. Canoes should not be regarded as speedboats. The swiftness and kind of water that is to be traveled and the size of the canoe will determine the appropriate horsepower. Some extremely fast water in mountain rivers cannot be run with a light motor. If the motor is fixed in a straightforward position by tightening the steering-bearing clamp, and paddles are also used to assist the forward motion, many rapids, otherwise impassable, can be ascended. I have, on occasion, even added, along with the motor, a small section of "squaw" sail, and paddled besides, to expedite travel through difficult sections of fast water.

As you increase the weight and horsepower of your motor, be sure that your canoe can handle it, and take care that your equipment load has an ample low gravity point in rough water. Carry service tools, sheer pins, extra spark plugs, and—on a long, rough trip—an extra prop.

The impeller type of outboard motor, driven by dual jets of water instead of a blade propeller, is in the process of development. The makers of this unit argue the advantage on the basis that the jet assembly operates above the keel line, and allows the canoe to travel in very shallow water—over reefs, logs, and other obstructions that might foul up a regular propeller blade. An obstacle that clears the canoe clears the impeller assembly, for there is no projection of the motor below the canoe to catch weeds. Manufacturers say that they are now planning to supply these jet impellers for outboard motors with propellers, making the assemblies interchangeable. Manufacturers of standard propeller outboard motors argue that jet motors must be a great deal larger and heavier than the standard propeller motors to have the same power. The canoeist should apply these competitive factors for comparison when he selects a motor for his own particular travel.

CLOTHING

Eliminate leather boots and shoes; they are hazardous in a canoe and also become soggy on portage trails. I use the combination moosehide, Indian-tanned moccasins inside moccasin-rubbers for most of my canoe travel. The moccasin-rubbers are made in Canada on a last molded to form fit the moccasined foot—not to fit over a shoe. They are easily removed in a canoe to give a pleasant sense of foot freedom. On portage trails, there is a moccasinlike tactility with the moccasin-rubber combination that is delightful. Wear wool socks in all seasons.

A pullover type, below-knee-length rain shirt; a sou'-wester hat; and a pair of lightweight, four-buckle overshoes have been the best combination for protection against rain that I have found. Overshoes left unbuckled in a canoe can readily be kicked off in an emergency. Ordinarily, such overshoes when worn over conventional

shoes are clumsy and large, but when worn over socks
are greatly reduced in size, and become small, light, and
springy footwear for canoe travel. Because the lightweight overshoe does not come in higher lengths than
four-buckle, I wear a pair of thin, rubberized, slipover
cuffs that are tied under the knee with a cord, and drape
over the overshoe.

The two-piece rain pants and jacket combination is an
abomination. These garments cause excessive condensation, and the pants are almost impossible to put on and
take off in a canoe—especially where this is frequently
necessary during sporadic rains. It must be recognized
that any rubberized or other impervious material that does
not "breathe" will cause condensation. The loose-fitting,
below-knee, so-called rain shirt, however, eliminates a
great deal of this condensation. Using the sou'wester hat instead of the rain shirt hood gives additional air circulation.
When the overshoes are worn unbuckled, their tops flared
wide open while you are seated in the canoe—the rain
shirt draping over them for protection—ventilation
reaches the whole body quite well, including even the
feet, thus reducing condensation considerably.

Most canoe voyagers eventually get around to wearing
lightweight wool underwear. The clammy feel of cotton
on wet, cold days usually decides the issue. The two-piece
style is my choice; the shirt, a crew neck, pullover type.
Much of the time, the only upper garment I wear is the
undershirt. I try to get it in red so that it looks like an
outer garment—and it shows up well in color photography.

A wool, stagged, outer shirt; a high-count, thin cotton
windbreaker; wool pants with knitted wool cuffs; and a

felt hat give ample change for most weather in canoe travel. The felt hat and windbreaker should be sprayed with aerosol cravenetting fluid—obtainable in any hardware or sporting goods store—a process which makes these items water resistant, not waterproof. (Waterproofing would create a condensation problem.) Such processing will ward off light showers, and save unpacking the rain equipment.

Specialized canoe equipment and provisions for wilderness travel are not always readily available in many parts of the continent. Also, there is often confusion concerning selection. If the reader will address his inquiries to me through the publisher, enclosing a self-addressed, stamped envelope, I will have the firms handling such items communicate directly with the reader. Inquiries should not be general, but refer to specific items. Also, if the reader has problems which he finds difficult to solve, I will be glad to contribute whatever information I can.

INFORMATIONAL

APPENDIX

THE following list is designed for a canoe journey of one month, where weather cannot be predicted. The list can be adapted to shorter or longer periods by inspection of each item for proportionate deletions or additions, based on wear and consumption, as applied to socks, flashlight batteries, insect spray, and so forth. The personal items are listed for each member of the party, the camping equipment for two members.

CLOTHING FOR ONE INDIVIDUAL

Long underwear, wool, medium weight	2 pairs of drawers
	1 undershirt (a substitute garment can be worn while the undershirt is being washed)
T-shirt and shorts (optional)	1 suit
Socks, wool, medium weight	4 pairs
Outer shirt, wool, lightweight	1
Pants, wool	1 pair
Belt or suspenders (braces)	1
Outer shirt, wool, stagged	1
Windbreaker, lightweight	1

Moccasins, preferably Indian-tanned moosehide, or buckskin, lightweight, to be worn over wool socks with moccasin-rubbers	2 pairs
Moccasin-rubbers (or ankle-height rubber camp mocs worn with socks only)	1 pair
Hat, felt, made water-repellent with aerosol cravenetting fluid	1
Bandanna handkerchief	1
Gloves, buckskin	1 pair
Rain shirt, below knee length	1
Sou'wester rain hat	1
Overshoes, 4-buckle, lightweight, worn directly over wool socks	1 pair
Rain pants cuffs, custom or homemade	1 pair

PERSONAL ITEMS

Wallet, in moisture-proof tobacco pouch	1
Watch, preferably pocket type	1
Compass, Cruiser type	1
Waterproof match safe	1
Matches (see Provision List)	
Belt knife, thin, 5- or 6-inch blade	1
Glasses, for vision, if needed, well cased	2 pairs
Toilet articles, including hand towel	1 set

Insect head net (in fly season)	1
Insect repellant, lotion or cream	1 bottle or tube
Diary and pencil	1 each
Map of region	1
Binoculars, compact type	1 pair
Life jacket (required by law in Canada)	

CAMP EQUIPMENT FOR TWO

Canoe	1
Paddles (including 1 spare required by law)	3
Tent, waterproof ground sheet, and mosquito net	1 each
Ropes for tent and tracking, No. 5 sash cord	300 feet
Aerosol insect tent spray in insect season	1 cylinder
Sleeping robe and air mattress	2 sets
Packsack and waterproof liner	2 sets
Pack basket, waterproof liner, and packsack	1 set
Tumpline or pack harness	1
Ax and sheath, ¾ size, single bit type	1
Whetstone, double-faced, combination fine and coarse India (small Arkansas slipstone, optional)	1 each
File, 6-inch, for roughing down nicked ax edge	1
Flashlight, extra bulbs, and batteries	1 set
Fishing equipment (greatly reduced amount)	1 set

Firearms and ammunition, if permitted (not legal in Canada outside of hunting season; not necessary as protection)	1 set
Camera equipment, including exposure meter, flash bulbs, and automatic shutter release	1 set
Outboard motor, if trip is to be motorized	1
Spare parts and tools for outboard motor	1 set
Canvas carrying case for motor	1
Gasoline mixed with oil for motor	Estimated for size of motor and length of trip
Gasoline (white) for primus stoves, or use patent fluids for this purpose	Estimated for length of trip and degree used

COOKING UTENSILS FOR TWO

Cooking pails (billies), nesting type	3	
Cups, stainless steel	2	Nested
Cereal bowls	2	and
Aluminum plates	2	packed in
Spoons	2	drawstring
Forks	2	bag
Frying pan with removable, long handle	1	
Pocket-size primus gasoline stove	1 or 2	
Reflector oven (optional if bannock baked in a frying pan is to be the bread used)	1	

Can opener	1
Dish towels	2
Sewing and repair kit (including canoe repair)	1 kit
First-aid items	1 kit
Toilet paper (see Provision Lists)	
Paper towels (optional)	1 or more rolls

FOR EXPEDITION TYPE OF JOURNEY
WITH CELESTIAL POSITION-FINDING EQUIPMENT

Light Explorer's transit or sextant and artificial horizon	1 set
Radio, small transistor type, combination standard and short wave, for navigation time signals	1
Plotting equipment: Mercator charts, protractor, divider, et cetera	1 set
Nautical Almanac or Ephemeris	1
H.O.214 Tables, for proper range of latitude	1

FOOD BUDGETS

Wilderness foods, processed for light weight, have had an interesting evolution. Pemmican and jerky were the earliest water-free foods that made travel into the deep interior possible with transported provisions. Pemmican is made by first cutting the fat from lean meat. The lean meat is then cut into long strips the size of a finger, and dried in the sun on pole racks. A small smoky fire is kept going on the windward side to keep off flies. When the lean meat is dry as bone—and about as hard—it is pounded into small flakes and then well mixed with the melted, refined fat (from which the cracklings have been removed) to form a solid mass. No salt is added, because salt draws moisture from the air, causing spoilage. The pemmican is sewed into skins for storage or transportation. Some has been made with the addition of dried berries and maple sugar, and other variations of enrichment. The most staple item is simply dried meat and fat, prepared as described. It keeps well in all seasons. It may be eaten raw, fried, boiled in stews, and otherwise prepared.

Sometimes the meat is dried as for pemmican and left in hard stick form, to be soaked for the cooking process, or munched in its dry, smoked form. The dry meat alone was called "jerky" by white explorers, and "kaspisāwan" by the Cree Indians.

The removal of water from various foods is not new. Indians dried berries and also wild roots which they sometimes ground into a flour for sundry uses. The real breakthrough for the canoe voyager came when dehydration of many foods became commercial practice. Some of the first dehydrated foods were unpalatable, having medicinal and other unpleasant flavors. Gradually they were improved, until now most are very acceptable.

The difficulty was that foods subjected to high temperatures for dehydration were modified, and also lost the true flavor of the original, fresh food item. Most of the vitamin value was lost. Some of these vitamins developed synthetically have been added to replace, or even increase, the natural vitamins.

No radical change took place over many years in dehydrated foods except the gradual improvement in process and taste. But in this last decade a significant discovery has been made in freeze-dried foods. Rapid freezing of various foods and the removal of moisture under low-temperature vacuum have allowed dehydration without much change in the physical or chemical properties of foods. Fresh meat, freeze-dried, is now made available for the canoe voyager during high temperatures throughout his trip. Steak—light in weight, retaining its original size and form —is reconstituted in 15 minutes of soaking in water. It can then be fried or broiled as regular steak. Stews also come prepared with this fresh, freeze-dried meat—the vegetables, likewise, being freeze-dried. Cooked, scrambled, freeze-dried eggs are made ready to eat by the addition of hot water poured into the foil envelope in which they are packed.

The canoe voyager has, thus, through the freeze-drying process, been able to alter his whole concept of provisioning; since what may be termed fresh foods will now, with freeze-dried items, replace some of the more common foods processed at high temperatures. Freeze-dried foods weigh about the same as common dehydrated foods, but they are bulkier, because the original shape and size are retained.

The following lists also contain the more common dehydrated foods. Weights in the lists are based on foods of the regular dehydrated type. You can best manage your provision list by first considering the food listed and then, where it is possible to substitute freeze-dried items, do so in the same approximate proportion of weight as the dehydrated foods listed.

Steaks, for example, weigh 2 ounces in their freeze-dried form. After 15 minutes of soaking, the time suggested by the packer, they weigh 6 ounces. The respective dry and reconstituted weights can be relative guides for both the fresh and canned meat in the following lists.

But do remember that the miracle of freeze-drying still has not wholly replaced freshly cut steaks or other meats. Where fresh meat can be carried for a short time on a trip, and weight doesn't matter, fresh meat should, of course, be used. This also applies to fresh fruit and vegetables. There is no point in being confined to dried foods for the average short trip.

Provision Lists

Two provision lists will be shown—one for longer journeys, when the fare is reduced to water-free, dehydrated, and freeze-dried foods in part; the other for shorter trips when common, domestic, fresh raw foods are suggested. I have based the amounts on approximately 4 pounds of food per man per day, when using the fresh, common, domestic foods; and approximately 2¼ pounds per man per day, of water-free and dehydrated foods. Where fish will be caught, this fresh supply can be cut to 3 pounds per man per day; and the 2¼ pounds of dry foods cut to 2. Substitutions, additions, and deletions, of course, will be made according to taste.

Pack all foods either in the combination polyethylene and cloth bag, or in press-on, friction-top cans coated inside with hot beeswax.

ONE-MONTH SUPPLY FOR TWO MEN—

REDUCED-WEIGHT FOODS, SUCH AS WATER-FREE, DEHYDRATED,

FREEZE-DRIED, AND CANNED, COOKED MEATS

	Pounds
Flour, white, including prepared biscuit mix and pancake flour	32
Cereals, such as quick-cooking and instant oatmeal, rice, et cetera	17
Hardtack, Ry-Krisp, sea biscuits	2
Potatoes, instant flakes and dehydrated pieces	9
Vegetable soup mixes, dehydrated, including dehydrated onions, or use small whole regular onions	9
Freeze-dried vegetable beef stew	2
Tomato paste	1
Macaroni	3
Dried fruit, such as apples, apricots, prunes, pears, peaches, raisins	9
Jam	5
Orange and lemon powder for citrus drink	3
Milk, powdered, whole	8
Eggs, dehydrated	4
Scrambled freeze-dried eggs	2
Peanut butter	2
Butter or oleomargarine (oleomargarine keeps better, but certain butter in sealed tins keeps well)	5

Vegetable shortening, including oleo-margarine	5
Canned meats, including ham, chicken, beef, pork, Canadian bacon, freeze-dried steak	15
Side bacon, fresh ham, and bologna to start	5
Cheese, fresh to start, then cheese spread and dry grated cheese	5
Instant coffee	2
Instant tea	½
or	
Leaf tea	1
Cocoa	1
Baking powder (omit if only commercial mixes are used)	1
Dry granule yeast (omit if no long stops are to be made for yeast bread, or if no sourdough items are to be prepared)	2
Salt	2
Pepper	½ ounce
Cinnamon	½ ounce
Vanilla	1 ounce
Seasoning salt	4 ounces
Vitamin tablets	4 ounces
Detergent (in cloth bag)	2 pounds
Toilet paper	4 rolls
Matches, large, wood (repacked in friction-top can)	1 box
Paper towels	2 rolls

ONE-WEEK SUPPLY FOR TWO MEN—
STANDARD HOUSEHOLD FOODS

Bread	5	loaves
Butter	2	pounds
Shortening and oleomargarine for cooking	2	pounds
Instant tea	¾	ounce
Instant coffee	12	ounces
or		
Ground coffee	2	pounds
Milk, dry, whole	1	pound
Sugar	2	pounds
Eggs, fresh, packed in friction-top can with oatmeal for buffer, or broken and put into friction-top wax-lined can	1½	dozen
Bacon, side, and Canadian	3	pounds
Steak, fresh	1¼	pounds
Steak, freeze-dried	1	pound
Ham	2½	pounds
Sausage, cured, bologna, etc.	1	pound
Canned meat	3	cans
Cheese, fresh and cheese spread	2	pounds
Canned beans, with pork, wieners, or hamburgers	3	cans
Fresh vegetables	5	pounds
Citrus fruit powder	½	pound
or		
Whole oranges	1	dozen
Dry soup mixes	4	envelopes

Peanut butter	1	pound
Dried fruit	2	pounds
Jam	2	pounds
Oatmeal (see eggs)	2	pounds
Pancake flour	2	pounds
Biscuit mix	2	pounds
Crackers	1	pound
Cookies	2	pounds
Potatoes, fresh, raw	3	pounds
Potatoes, instant	1	pound
Onions, fresh, raw	1	pound
Pepper	½	ounce
Mustard	1	jar
Salt	1	pound
Pickles	1	jar
Toilet paper	2	rolls
Paper towels	1	roll
Matches, repacked into friction- top can	1	large box

Some items of food omitted from the above list may seem important. For example, we have lived so traditionally with the common, dry, navy bean that its addition to the food budget seems to be a foregone conclusion. Yet it takes hours to cook this bean; and unless it has previously been "precooked," or processed to become "instant," it is not a practical item for canoe travel.

Most travel in the wilderness gets reduced to what I like to term "expeditious expeditions." Food lists suited to permanent camps, or to a wilderness cabin, therefore, must be revised for canoe travel to insure the greatest possible convenience in packing and preparation.

The list given will allow a wide range of meals. The important thing is to experiment for variety. Breadstuffs, baked in a reflector oven, or a bannock in a frypan propped up before an open fire can be given great variety by mixing the plain doughs and then adding various precooked cereals to the white flour; or, adding whole dried milk, dried egg, dried fruit, and sugar for a coffee-cake type of bread.

A basic item that will span a variety of meals is cream sauce or white sauce, which will allow you to cream fish, dried beef, ham, canned chicken, and many other items for serving on hot baking powder biscuits. Any cookbook will have cream sauce recipes, but where they call for liquid milk and whole eggs, you will add dehydrated ingredients. A cream sauce in a dry mix, which needs only water and cooking, can thus be carried.

It is rather pointless to mix ingredients at every meal when they can be mixed in advance, or where commercial mixes provide even better results. Always cut back every operation in advance of the trip by any possible preliminary mixing. And give careful consideration to commercially prepared mixes.

Breadstuffs, such as biscuits, bannock, coffee bread, pancakes, cookies, cake, cobblers, loaf bread, and pie, can readily be baked outdoors in a reflector oven. Sourdough has been the basic rising agent for centuries, but has lost its popular use with the development of so many commercial bread mixes. It is, however, a very healthful and expedient way to make bread. For sourdough: Mix a quart of lukewarm water, an envelope of yeast, a tablespoon of sugar (no salt); add enough flour to make a thick batter. The yeast works on the sugar, and after

Folding Reflector Oven Does the Baking Job

three days in a warm, not hot, place, when the stock will be ready, it will smell yeasty and somewhat alcoholic.

To a cup of this fermented batter, placed in a mixing pan, add about a third of a teaspoon of baking soda. This is the only fussy part of making good sourdough. If you get too much soda in the stock, you can taste the soda; if you do not get enough, the breads will be heavy. Experiment. Chemically changed by the addition of the soda, the sourdough now gives you a "sweetened" basic rising agent for whatever you wish to make.

For pancakes: Add to a cup of the sourdough mixture: 1 tablespoon of melted shortening, 2 of dry milk, 1 of dry egg, another of sugar, ½ teaspoon salt, ½ cup flour, and sufficient water to make a pancake batter. Use part cake flour, if you have it, for tenderer pancakes. Pour the batter into a uniformly hot, lightly greased frypan. A burned-down wood fire of glowing coals is needed for this —no flame.

For sourdough bannock (bread baked in a frying pan) use the pancake mixture, but one less rich, and mix the dough just stiff enough so that you can cut a lump of dough out of the mixing pan and knead it in your hands. Use fat on your hands instead of flour to prevent sticking. Flatten it well in a frypan, then prop it up about eight inches, or less, from an active flame fire. For lighter bannock, let rise in a warm place before baking.

The preparation of a typical, simple bannock is a unique process. Open the bag of biscuit mix wide. With your fist form a hollow in the mix. Pour water into the hollow, and stir with a stick. When a lump of dough forms, pick it out of the bag, knead between the hands a few moments, then flatten and place in the frying pan for baking. Prop up the bannock pan about eight inches from an open flame-type fire. As the bannock browns, turn it over and prop up the other side until it, too, is brown. Biscuits made in a reflector oven should be placed the same distance from the flame fire.

If you will swab the surface of any breadstuffs with a solution of dry egg and water before you bake them, the color, richness of crust, and flavor will be much improved. Baking various breads is the most avoided part of outdoor cooking—and needlessly so. Once you have mastered it—a rather simple process—you are well along toward becoming a good outdoor cook. (For a complete treatment of camp cooking, see my book, *The New Way of the Wilderness*, The Macmillan Company.)

The following items are a few suggestions of what can be prepared with the first food list in this appendix. Stand-

Pan-Baking the Traditional Bannock

ard household items in the second list can be substituted for those in the first list.

Oatmeal mush with rich, reconstituted, whole milk powder and sugar. Oatmeal mush with cooked dry fruit, milk and sugar.

Boiled rice with milk and sugar. Rice pudding.

Potatoes, mashed; potato patties; fried, reconstituted, dehydrated potatoes.

Vegetable soup from reconstituted, dried vegetables, and any of the meats.

Fresh fried fish.

Vegetable and meat stew.

Freeze-dried stew.

Macaroni and cheese, using cheese spread or dry, grated cheese.

Macaroni and tomato sauce, using tomato paste and reconstituted dried onions.

Fruit sauce from dried apples, apricots, prunes, and so forth.

Cobblers from dried fruit with piecrust dough for top.

Orange juice from reconstituted orange powder.

Whole milk beverage from reconstituted dry milk. Whenever time and temperature permit, mix the dry milk with water and let it stand for 12 hours. This will greatly improve the flavor.

Peanut butter, jam, and butter with bread.

Ham, chicken, beef, pork, Canadian bacon, and freeze-dried steak either with potatoes, instant rice, or creamed over hot biscuits.

Scrambled, freeze-dried eggs.

Coffee.

Tea.

Cocoa.

Writing this section, I think of a Cree friend with whom I traveled early in the century. I wonder what he would think about the modern-day luxury of this food budget. We had a canoe, fishline, rifle, two rabbitskin blankets, flour, tea, and a bag of salt. We slept under the canoe, and lived largely off the country—on fish, game, and berries. Life was a lot less complicated. Looking back nostalgically, it seems that we felt more closely, more vibrantly, the pulse of the earth.